Make Your Own Preschool Games

Other Books by Sally Goldberg, Ph.D.

Baby and Toddler Learning Fun

Constructive Parenting

Parenting Involvement Begins at Birth

Make Your Own Preschool Games

A Personalized
Play and Learn Program

Sally Goldberg, Ph.D.

PERSEUS
PUBLISHING

Cambridge, Massachusetts

Library of Congress Control Number: 2002104500

ISBN 1-55561-344-6

Perseus Publishing books are available at special discounts for bulk purchases in the United States by corporations, institutions, and other organizations. For more information, please contact the Special Markets Department at the Perseus Books Group, 11 Cambridge Center, Cambridge, MA 02142, or call (617)252-5298.

Perseus Publishing is a member of the Perseus Books Group.

Set in 12-point Goudy by the Perseus Books Group.

Illustrations by Cathie Lowmiller.

First printing, May 2002
1 2 3 4 5 6 7 8 9 10 – 05 04 03 02

Find Perseus Publishing on the World Wide Web at
http://www.perseuspublishing.com

To my daughters Cynthia and Deborah. Cynthia helped me develop the games. Deborah helped me refine them. Then Cynthia and Deborah grew up to become wonderful young women and great friends to me and to each other.

Contents

Part Four: Language Development 153

Part Five: The Home Environment 207

Foreword

Young children are busy, busy, busy! They are interested in everything around them. Your three, four, or five year old wants to touch everything, explore the surroundings, and investigate the how and why of items in the environment. You have a unique opportunity. Children not only want to please their parents, but use them as a model for everything they do. They mimic and copy your movements. They are interested in the things you find intriguing. This puts families in a special, advantageous position. As you nurture and love your growing child, you also become their first teacher. Dr. Sally Goldberg has taken this benefit and gives you multiple examples of how to expand your child's knowledge while providing that necessary one-on-one time that every child needs.

In the 1990s scientists were able to document what early-care educators have known for decades. The first years are the learning years! Nearly 90 percent of all brain growth occurs in the first five years of life. The quality of the child's environment and the variety of experiences help the child reach full potential. Knowledge is acquired from the interaction of the child's senses with the sights, sounds, and smells in his or her surroundings. Nestled quietly in the research is the role of parents. Adults enhance the experience with descriptive language. They help define the early years. A safe, loving atmosphere helps open the pathways to learning. Children develop their lifelong attitude about learning.

In the book, *Make Your Own Preschool Games*, Dr. Goldberg gives multiple ideas to help your child grow physically, cognitively, and socially as he acquires language. The most positive outgrowth of this approach is the close relationship you will establish with your child. Spending minutes that focus on your child each day can only be beneficial. This interaction in the early years should translate into an open communication avenue as your child matures. This mutual understanding is the kind that will last through the years. And to think it only takes a small investment of time and materials when your child is young!

How refreshing to know you can make a difference in your child's readiness for formal, academic learning! Imagine how simple it is to gather household items to create learning games. Listening to advertising and marketing hype, we are lulled into thinking expensive, high-technology toys and games are best for educating children; but the flashing lights and battery-powered movement are not as exciting to children as to adults. They quickly lose interest in them. That old adage that children like the boxes better than the contents is often true. Simplicity is often best. Your few minutes playing these games with your child is not only more productive, but is also strengthening the bonds so necessary for self-esteem. You will reap rewards, not just watching the growth, but in the close relationship you establish with your child.

Sitting for hours in front of the television or watching videos is a passive activity. Children can't learn new skills, exercise muscles, or utilize their reasoning power. There is no expansion of communication skills. Selecting a game and playing directly with their parent is a better choice.

Young children are never bored. This is an adult concept. When children tire of an activity, they seek another. Ever watch children in a restaurant? They squirm and wiggle, but all the time they are exploring the silverware, the floor, the chair, their clothes, the salt and pepper shakers, or whatever they can reach. What a perfect time to snatch a few moments and do an activity from this book. Using a game that your child knows well and enjoys participating in will allow both of you to pass the time quickly. It will prevent "out-of-control" behavior from escalating into a situation that requires discipline. Instead you will create a positive parent-child moment.

Children love repetition, and it is actually beneficial. Repeating activities helps put the skills into your child's permanent memory. By playing the same games repeatedly, children acquire mastery. Combining your creativity with Dr. Goldberg's suggested games, you can repeat the activities in a variety of settings with varied supplies.

Dr. Goldberg stresses that children need to make choices as to which game to pursue each day. Your flexibility allows your child to be in charge of his own learning. This empowerment helps children to feel good about themselves and their abilities.

Creating learning moments in your busy lives isn't difficult. Short interactive sessions with your child not only teaches basic skills, but helps to create satisfying family ties. There are many books about either child development or games for children; this book ties them together. Uniting parent and child, *Make Your Own Preschool Games* is a valuable tool.

Suzanne Gellens, M.S.
Executive Director
Early Childhood Association of Florida

Preface

When my second daughter, Deborah, was born in February 1981, everyone asked, Are you going to do the same educational activities with her that you did with your first daughter? At that time the answer to that question was unknown. I did not know for sure what I would do until it came time to doing it. As it turned out, I chose to do everything and more. Deborah had the advantage of having a whole play-and-learn program ready for her. From that early fun I had with my two girls grew, first, *Baby and Toddler Learning Fun*, and now *Make Your Own Preschool Games*.

When my first daughter, Cynthia, was three, I began collecting more and more information about valuable activities to do with her. I made lists, but the more I studied the longer my lists became. At that point I could see that the activities began to center themselves on categories. Then I wrote out the games for each category on a separate sheet so that I could easily add new ideas. This new way enabled me to keep track of what I was doing with her. I then put each of the games on an index card and grouped them by category. By putting each game on a card and showing her a group of cards from which she could pick, she got the sense of beginning, ending, and accomplishing a set of activities. In addition, she had the fun of choosing what activity we were going to do together. The identifying category symbols became a learning experience itself. For example, one category of game we identified as the "?" games.

By the time my daughter was six years old, the whole system of *Make Your Own Preschool Games* had become quite solidified. Whenever we had free time together, she would say, "Mom, let's do the games." The amount of time we worked at it varied. If we had fifteen minutes, we would do only a few. With more time, we would do more. It did not matter; the important part was that we both had direction in spending playtime together in a satisfying and productive way.

Four years later this home-activity system developed from lists and index cards and became the original *Make Your Own Preschool Games* book published in 1986. It was complete with 124 activities. Now, fourteen years later, the original *Make Your Own Preschool Games* book has become this new edition, expanded to 168 games and updated with millennium materials and ideas. All of the original activities have been refined, and many new ones have been added. The original set of categories has been expanded, and the new one corresponds to specific areas of development. The card system is clearer in this book, and that makes the whole system easier to follow and more fun to use.

Acknowledgments

This second edition was generated right out of the first edition. New materials and a broader perspective about play and learning accounts for the differences. The content is a direct extension of *Baby and Toddler Learning Fun*. It provides the next step in the play-and-learn process.

Given all of that, the stature of this book rests on its heart. That is what comes from a positive association with close friends, family, and professionals. Thank you Carol and Bill Rascoe for expressing such love for me and my work. Thank you Beth Damon for being that genuine spirit so supportive of my hopes and dreams. Thank you cousins Barry Harrow and Ann Flood for your continued interest in my mission and your continued support for helping me carry it out. Thank you cousins Cookie and George Berman for your continued interest in my professional pursuits. Abundant thanks to Marnie Cochran, senior editor at Perseus Books, for believing in the value of this book. Cindy Randall, you are the brains and beauty behind it all.

If you like the drawings in this book, that is because they are terrific. Special thanks to Cathie Lowmiller who drew them and to Karen Koenig and her daughter Amanda who posed for all of the original photographs.

Introduction

Whereas *Baby and Toddler Learning Fun* is for children aged birth to three, *Make Your Own Preschool Games: A Personalized Play-and-Learn Program* is a guide for the three to five age group. This book takes over where the first one leaves off. At around three years of age, your child has an increased awareness of people and an increased interest in interacting with them. Whereas before his play was toy oriented, it has now become game centered and includes many different kinds of activities that involve other people. As you plan your child's daily schedule, keep in mind that a balance of both active and quiet forms of play will work best.

Throughout history, parents have been involved in their children's lives in different ways. Each generation of parents comes along and tries to improve upon the way their parents were with them. With the best of intentions, each new group has to deal with the parental responsibilities of the times and a different style of life.

We find today's parents extremely busy. Most of them lead the equivalent of three full-time jobs—earning money, parenting, and taking care of a household. Many others carry the additional responsibility of taking college-level courses leading to bachelors or higher degrees, or some other professional development qualification.

Given that situation, many parents today have a limited amount of time to spend with their own children. Some have only enough time to attend to the bare necessities of feeding, clothing, and providing a home for their child. Others have limited time but are able to round up a little bit more to provide an enriched learning environment. A few are able to give large amounts of time to making sure that their preschooler is happily engaged in productive, educationally stimulating activities for most of the time.

No matter what your situation, it is helpful for you to know what is considered a well-rounded supplementary educational program for your child. It is also helpful for you to have the recommended games and activities presented in an easy-to-follow format that is effective and enjoyable.

The way this book is set up is the key to its usability. For a child with a learning disability or a delay, you can easily find a game or category of games that will be especially beneficial to your child's development. For an advanced child, you can choose specific games for enrichment. For any child, you can feel confident that the games to choose from will foster continued developmental growth. Each of the games is designed to help your child grow in at least one area.

About the Games

Because the designed and selected games for this book have a creative aspect to them, they can be tailored to the ability and personality of your child. Each game has an objective that can be met by a personalized version of the game. The same game can be used repeatedly with more numbers, harder words, more difficult drawings, and so on. Your child will grow with the games, and the games will grow with your child. This is a unique and efficient style of play. What you will see will be your child "growing with the games."

The same games can be used with two different children, each enjoying the task in the same or different appropriate ways. Being able to repeat the games is an important part of their effectiveness. Most of the games are designed from available household items or no materials at all. They demonstrate how to use (in an educational way) many items you already have.

There is also a section on the home environment, which includes information about teaching your child at home and working with teachers. The hours your child spends at home and with you can be productive. There are many educational activities that you can do almost any time and almost anywhere. The key to parent teaching is that much of it can be done through a games format. The hours children spend in a preschool classroom are also important. Because many children spend many hours in that kind of setting, it is also important to have a perspective on that. What to expect and what not to expect will help you as you continue to play the vital role of parent to your child.

Topics and Categories

For this age group the educational topics are all the developmental areas—cognitive, motor, social, and language. These topics break down into categories in this way:

I. Cognitive
   a. Mathematics
   b. Science
   c. Social Studies

II. Motor
    a. Gross Motor
    b. Fine Motor
    c. Midline
III. Social
    a. Social Skills
    b. Art
    c. Music
    d. Drama
IV. Language
    a. Reading
    b. Writing
    c. Listening
    d. Speaking

These are foundation skills for later learning. They follow the prerequisite skills of self-awareness, colors, letters, numbers, shapes, and beginning reading as described in *Baby and Toddler Learning Fun*. Since you may feel that some of the games are more appropriate for your child than others, and since your child will show preference as well, there is flexibility in this kind of program. The idea is to turn many routine parent-child interactions into positive supportive experiences.

Using the Cards

Each of the chapters that follows explains the games for one of the categories. In the back of this book is a list of all the games that can be made into a set of cards organized by category. There should be one card for each game. Each card should have the name of the game and the page number on which it is explained on one side, and the name of the category on the other side. You can make your own set of cards by using three-by-five-inch index cards, one card for each game.

When you are ready to play the games from one of the categories, all the cards from that category should be laid out on a table, category side up, in front of you and your child. Learning to read the category itself will be a learning experience for your child. Once the cards are laid out, any kind of appropriate counting or mathematical activity can be played with the cards even before your child actually selects a card for play. When ready, your child may choose a game for play. When he picks up his card, he can first name the category on one side of the card and then try to read, to the best of his ability, the title of the game on the other side of the card. You can help with this reading activity as well. Being able to select a game in this way from a series of cards adds an element of surprise to the game.

Once your child chooses a game, you or your child can gather whatever materials you need to play the game. Some of the games need few or no materials at all. Others need several materials. Some of the games are short and take almost no time. Others are extensive and take quite a long time. The short games will give your child an immediate feeling of accomplishment. The longer ones will give your child the feeling he has shared an in-depth play-together time with you. Because you will know quickly and easily from the game description the objective behind each activity, you will feel satisfied that you have spent playtime with your child in an enriching way. In addition, because of the variety of categories and also because of the variety of games in each of the categories, you can feel relaxed that your child will be getting a mix of important developmental play experiences.

Select a game.

When you finish all the games in one category, you can lay out the cards for another. If you go through the categories in order, it will take quite a lot of time to get back to any one category again. This type of rotation will make all the games in any one category seem new and interesting again. It will reduce your need for going out to buy new games.

A Personalized, Flexible Program

If your child has a weakness or an interest in one particular category, you can play the games in that category more frequently. While it is not necessary for your child to go through all the games in a category, that might be exactly what your child wants to do. In addition, your child might not want to play a particular game on one day but then decide to play it on another. This approach, which offers much flexibility, is designed to meet the needs of each individual child. You will never feel you are trying to fit your child into a specific program. This whole system of games is designed to be tailored to your child's own uniqueness.

Another advantage to playing these games is that most of the materials used are easily accessible household items. That makes the games inexpensive and easy to play. In addition, you will be able to play these games at many other times during the day, even when a special playtime is not planned. For example, you can repeat at bathtime a game like the fine-motor activity of wringing out a washcloth. Therefore, the formal game time can become a reminder for activities that you can do as part of other routine daily activities.

Many of the activities that we have isolated out today as beneficial, educationally stimulating activities are related to natural family life of yesteryear. In the old days when families lived closer together, grandparents, aunts, uncles, and cousins were around to play a major role in the child care of the very young. These relatives talked to their kin often, recited nursery rhymes, and read them stories, all natural ways to develop language. Later as children grew and learned skills of the home and family work, they helped out with that work. Much of it helped them develop in all four areas of development:

- Cognitive
- Motor
- Social
- Language

These home experiences naturally introduced them to similar kinds of activities that now make up the categories in this book:

    I. Mathematics
   II. Science
  III. Social Studies
  IV. Gross Motor
   V. Fine Motor
  VI. Midline
 VII. Social Skills
VIII. Art
  IX. Music
   X. Drama
  XI. Reading
 XII. Writing
XIII. Listening
XIV. Speaking

This whole process was educationally stimulating and naturally led to the development of productive individuals.

Movement

Movement is especially important for young children. It is developmentally appropriate, stimulating, and enjoyable. Children are mobile and become happy when they have the opportunity to move around. They become unhappy when they find themselves confined to one particular place for an extended period of time. The younger the child, the greater percentage of movement time is necessary. It is no surprise that toddlers resist being in car seats. While it is absolutely necessary for them to travel in appropriate car-seat restraints, they are not comfortable when they cannot move around for long periods of time.

Swinging.

Movement starts in the womb. A mother-to-be can feel that easily. As she walks or even rocks in a rocking chair, her unborn baby is quieted and relaxed. Then after her baby is born, she can notice the constant movement.

When you rock your baby and provide him with gentle bounces, you see your new baby smile and laugh. When your baby gets a little older, holding him as you walk or taking him for a ride in a carriage or stroller once again provides him with pleasure. Next, when he learns to walk, you find your toddler always on the go. Now, as a preschooler, he will want to help you with your work, play vigorously with toys, and be active out-of-doors, swinging on swings and climbing on all kinds of playground equipment.

Curiosity

Young children have inborn curiosity that guides them in their play. They will naturally seek out opportunities to explore and at the same time exercise their bodies. For example, age-old games like hide-and-seek, Simon Says, and playing catch with a simple ball appear generation after generation. Newly developed mechanical toys and the most recent technological revolution in millennium toys are valuable when used in the right way, at the right time, and in the right place; but they should never replace hands-on, creative play experiences with materials like sand, water, clay or play dough, blocks, and bubbles, and important run-and-jump activities.

Learning Problems and Early Learning Experiences

Today we have a large population of children with learning disabilities. They have average to above average intelligence but have learning difficulties in one or more of these areas—reading, writing, listening, speaking, or mathematics. Also common are children with Attention Deficit Disorder (ADD) and Attention Deficit Hyperactivity Disorder (ADHD). Many of these children also have normal intelligence but experience major learning difficulties because of their inability to concentrate for long periods of time. A rapidly growing theory is that many of these problems relate back to a lack of appropriate stimulation activities during their early experiences. The fault is not with parents or with home life but with our whole change to such a mechanically and technologically fast-paced style of life.

In this book, as well as in *Baby and Toddler Learning Fun*, you will find a wide range of basic activities that have been either selected or designed to provide your child with important experiences related to basic learning skills and abilities. They are ones that can be individualized and shaped for your own child. Knowing what your child already experiences in his life, you can help your child choose others that will round out his experiences. Working with your child to select from this wide range of activities, you can feel confident that you will expose your child to important growth opportunities that might otherwise have been overlooked. These basic activities are all intrinsically fun and work well with children of all abilities, interests, and backgrounds.

Each of Parts One through Four covers an area of development. Each of the areas is explained briefly so that you will know important information about it. Then within each area you will see the topics that are related to that area. Those topics along with their subtopics are also briefly explained so that you will have broader information about the games when you play them. With an understanding of the topics and subtopics you will be better able to make up more games that will be fun and worthwhile for your child to experience. For example,

Part One is the cognitive development area. The topics under it are mathematics, science, and social studies. The subtopics in the area of mathematics are number sense, measurement, geometry and spatial sense, algebra, and data analysis and probability.

PART ONE

Cognitive Development

Cognitive development refers to learning about the world. Through experiencing the environment in different ways and then developing an understanding of those experiences, there is learning. All learning takes place through the five senses.

The more of the five senses that are being used, the more impact the learning situation will have. A good example is the beach. You experience it as something to see, to hear, to touch, to taste, and to smell. You can see the sights, hear the waves and people, touch the sand and water, taste the food, and smell the sea and other aromas. You experience the entire atmosphere on many levels. You also remember it well because of these strong sensory impressions.

These are powerful learning years. Children at this age continue to develop skills and abilities that emanate from curiosity and discovery. They are in the process of learning to do all kinds of things—express themselves with language, build with blocks and other materials, and create in all kinds of different ways.

What is important is what is happening at the time. Preschool children are not thinking about the past or pondering the future. If an activity is taking place, your child will want to participate in it. If another child has an interesting toy, your child will want to play with it too.

Hands-on activities and experiences hold the key to cognitive development. Explain, teach, and let your child experience as much as possible during these years. Remember this well-known rule of thumb: People remember 10 percent of what they hear, 50 percent of what they see, and 90 percent of what they experience.

At this stage you will be able to set up activities with your child that have simple rules to follow. As your child progresses, the rules and instructions for play can become more complicated and extensive. The Why? and How? stages are part of this picture. Your inquisitive child will seek information from you. Whenever possible, be there to explain what is going on, how things work, and the reasons for many different rules and regulations.

Cognitive development refers to learning. No child can learn too much. Just as each child born is a container for love, a container that can be continually filled and always have room for more, so is each child a container for knowledge, the same kind of container that can be continually filled and always have room for more. Feel free to continue to fill these containers day in and day out. Your child will benefit from everything you do.

The categories for this topic are mathematics, science, and social studies. These three areas of study provide the basis for understanding the world in which we live. They are all avenues of inquiry that we are drawn to explore in nature: Mathematics provides important structural concepts for many different areas of life—building, categorizing, storing, money, measurement, and even probability and statistics. Science delves into the physical nature of our universe. It tells us what the world is made of and how it works in both a physical and a natural way.

Social studies is all about people. Through psychological and sociological endeavors, we learn what people are like, what they are capable of doing on their own, and how they live together in groups. All of these areas of study can and should be presented to preschoolers on the simplest level as preparation for further study on more advanced levels.

1

$$\begin{array}{ccc} 1 & 2 & 3 \\ 4 & 5 & 6 \\ 7 & 8 & 9 \\ & 10 & \end{array}$$

Games for Mathematics

Preparing children to be comfortable with the world of numbers is important. It is a complex area of study that is basic to modern life. It is a little like a language, with concepts, theories, and systems that play a role in learning about the world. No matter how technologically advanced we become and no matter how much of our mathematical activities can be taken over by computers, we will always need to know mathematics. Number sense, measurement, geometry and spatial sense, algebraic thinking, and data analysis and probability all play a role in daily living. The more we can prepare our children in these areas of study, the richer and more successful their lives will be.

Children who understand the basics of mathematics will know that numbers denote a measurement of magnitude (how big), of distance (how far), and of quantity (how many). This understanding relates to the ability to perceive size, comprehend that numbers have stable values, and know that they are always either smaller or bigger than other numbers and by the same amounts.

The term "mathematics" is defined in the *American Heritage Dictionary of the English Language* (p. 1110) as: "The study of the measurement, properties, and relationships of quantities, using numbers and symbols."

The following games have been taken from these areas of study:

Number Sense—Number sense is understanding the relative sizes of numbers and how to use them.

Measurement—Measurement is determining length, area, volume, money, time, and other quantities.

Geometry and Spatial Sense—Geometry and spatial sense includes identifying shapes and understanding their various attributes.

Algebra—Algebra is an area of arithmetic in which letters of the alphabet represent numbers and there is an analysis of patterns, relations, symbols, and classification.

Data Analysis and Probability—Data analysis includes collecting and interpreting information. Probability is determining the likelihood that something will happen.

Number Sense

1. Ten Little Numbers

Objective: To teach your child number sense and number concepts from one to ten.

About the Game: Using sheets of paper, make number charts like the ones in the illustration. If you have a set of ten stick-on numbers, use them on a chart. If you can find stick-on stars and stick-on dots, often available in office supply stores, use those as well. If you have any sets of ten things, you can also use those for counting in this activity. Connecting this simple tune with numerals, stars, dots, and other objects will do much to enhance your child's number sense.

How to Play: Each time you sing "The Ten Little Numbers," point to one of the groupings and count each item in the group as you say each number. Here are the words to sing to the tune of "Ten Little Indians."

1 little, 2 little, 3 little numbers,
4 little, 5 little, 6 little numbers,
7 little, 8 little, 9 little numbers,
10 little numbers on the chart.

Change the word "numbers" to stars, dots, paper clips, or whatever you are counting. Traditionally this song has been used for counting our ten fingers. When you do that, notice what a good finger exercise it is as each finger is raised one at a time.

2. Find the Number

Objective: To teach your child number sense and number concepts from one to ten.

About the Game: By playing a manipulative game, your child will see that any particular number is always in the same position

Ten little numbers.

on the number line. Your child will have many hands-on experiences with these cards and therefore grow in his knowledge of number concepts.

How to Play: Use two sets of ten three-by-five-inch index cards numbered from one to ten with large clear numerals on them. Draw or use stick-on dots to place the corresponding number of dots on the back of each card. Place one set of cards in a line on a table, number side up in ascending order. Mix up the second set of cards and place them in a pile, number side up.

Have your child draw the first card from the pile and say the number on it. Tell him to find the match on the number line of cards and to place it on top of the match. Take your turn and continue to play until all the cards from the pile have been matched correctly.

A more advanced version of the game is to match the dots sides of the cards to the number line of cards. In addition, you can use the number side of the cards to match to a dot-side number line. You can also make more of these cards and continue the game with cards up to twenty.

Carrying this game to the highest level, you can place one set of cards out to be a number line and then set up two sets of the dots cards from one to five in a pile. Then take turns with your child picking two dots cards at a time. Count the dots on the two cards together and then place them on the correct number card on the number line.

Measurement

3. Measure It

Objective: To teach your child the beginning concept of measuring.

About the Game: By using a simple ruler, you child will get the idea that items exist in different lengths. By referring to the terms "feet," "inches," and "centimeters," your child will become familiar with basic linear measurement terms. This skill will lead to the ability to use linear measurement for problem solving.

How to Play: Take turns finding objects in the room that are straight. First you name one, and then have your child measure it with a twelve-inch ruler. Then have him name one, and you measure it with the ruler. Here are some examples of items you may find to measure:

- Table
- Shelf

- Bookcase
- Book
- Window
- Door

You might also want to measure parts of your bodies like arms, legs, and actual feet. For a beginning measurer, measure only in feet. If the item is more than one, two, or three feet even, say it is *a little more than* one, two, or three feet. For a more experienced measurer, you can point out the extra inches or centimeters.

4. Weigh It

Objective: To teach your child the beginning concept of weighing.

About the Game: Find empty containers that are exactly the same. A good place to look is in the recycle bin. Here are some examples of what you might find:

- Plastic containers in any size.
- Plastic bottles in any size.
- Plastic or Styrofoam take-home containers.

Then fill one of a matched pair and leave one empty. Here are some substances for fillers:

- Rice
- Dry beans
- Paper clips

This introduction to weight as a measurement will expand your child's awareness of measuring with a purpose.

How to Play: Take turns holding each one of the matched pair containers. As you lift each one, identify one as heavy and one as light. Then if you have a scale handy, weigh each one. Show your child the weight as it appears on the scale. A bath-room scale is handy for this activity. You can also use an inexpensive scale from an office supply store, the kind used for weighing packages to be sent by mail or to be shipped.

5. Money Containers

Objective: To teach your child the value of coins.

About the Game: Find any five containers with lids. You will probably find your recycle bin a good place to look for these. Cut small coin-size slits in the lids. Then label each of the five containers with a different coin name and its value. Suggested are stick-on labels that are available in office supply stores. Then put together a collection of small change.

How to Play: Take turns picking a coin from a group on the table and placing it in the correct container. For example, a dime should go in the container marked "dime 10c" and a nickel should go in the one labeled "nickel 5c." As you and your child take turns picking each coin and placing it in each correct slot, say the name of the coin and its value.

For a more advanced version of the activity, open the filled containers of coins. Take turns selecting coins from two different containers and saying their value as added together.

6. Time Clocks

Objective: To teach your child beginning time-telling skills.

About the Game: Use simple nine-inch white paper plates, colored three-by-five-inch index cards, and brass closures. While you can easily find these paper plates in any grocery store, you can find the index cards and brackets in an office supply store.

How to Play: Cut a half-inch strip off the long side of an index card and then cut a half-inch strip off the short side of the same index card. Then snip the corners off one end of each strip to make them look like the long hand and short hand of a clock. Use a bracket to attach the hands to a paper plate. Then add numbers from 1 to 12 to the plate to make a simple clock.

Have fun making times for your child that represent different "o'clock" times. After your child is comfortable with this activity, ask him to make times for you to identify. Feel free to progress to more complicated times as your child is ready. The half-past times like 1:30, 6:30, and others should be next. After awhile you can even get to "quarter after" times. Eventually you can use this simple clock to teach time in five-minute sequences and by ones. There is no rush to get to these higher levels, but it is good to know that this simple technique provides a clear way to teach these concepts.

On the highest level you can use the index cards to write times on them. Eventually you will have a set of familiar times. Then you can take turns picking the times and making those times on the actual clock.

Telling time.

Geometry and Spatial Sense

7. Recognizing Shapes

Objective: To teach your child to recognize basic shapes.

About the Game: Circles, squares, and rectangles are all around. Triangles, hexagons, and other shapes are there too, but they are harder to find. This detective work will lay the initial groundwork for success in geometry.

How to Play: Start with a simple shape like a circle, square, or rectangle and make the activity into a treasure hunt. Take

There's a circle.

turns looking for examples of these items in your room. Here are some examples of circles to find:

- Plates
- Knobs
- Bottle caps
- Glasses
- Tables

Here are some squares:

- Windows
- CD cases
- Boxes
- Tables

Here are some rectangles:

- Doors
- Windows
- Books
- Tables

There are many items in these shapes. Some will be hard to find at first, but as you continue to look, you will continue to find more and more.

8. Drawing Shapes

Objective: To teach your child beginning shape recognition.

About the Game: You can start with beginning shapes with this activity, but you can advance to more difficult shapes with this game. This experience will initiate the start of a spacial sense.

How to Play: Fold a sheet of paper in four parts. In the top left-hand corner, draw a shape. Then have your child copy the shape in the box underneath it. Then in the top right-hand corner, have your child draw a shape for you to copy in the box underneath it. Use crayons to color in the shapes if you and your child wish. Using other sheets of paper, continue this activity as long as you both have interest in playing.

Algebra

9. Making Patterns

Objective: To teach your child to recognize and create simple patterns.

About the Game: Have fun finding different objects for this activity. This process lays the groundwork for future work in the field of algebra.

How to Play: Collect your materials for making patterns. Here are some examples:

- Paper clips in different sizes and different colors.
- Toothpicks in different colors.
- Plastic stirrers in different colors.
- Golf tees in different colors.

Start by making simple patterns for your child to copy. Next make a simple pattern and have your child continue it. Then encourage your child to make patterns for you to match and continue.

10. Tap a Pattern

Objective: To teach your child to hear patterns.

About the Game: Sound patterns are as important as visual patterns. They are related to future algebraic thinking.

How to Play: Start with three easy syllable taps. Here are some suggested variations:

- Long, short, short
- Long, long, short
- Long, long, long
- Short, short, long

You tap the pattern first. Then ask your child to tap it back. Ask your child to tap a pattern, and then you tap it back. A variation is to tap the syllables in your child's name. Then tap the syllables in yours. Tap the syllables in other people's names if you wish. As you get more and more used to this game, experiment with different patterns, clapping your hands, and using items like spoons, shakers, or bells.

Data Analysis and Probability

11. Graphing Results

Objective: To teach your child to read simple graphs.

About the Game: Look around your house for items to graph. Here are some suggestions:

- Colors of pairs of shoes.
- Numbers of different kinds of silverware.
- Colors of toothpicks, paper clips, golf tees, or stirrers.
- Colors of shirts, pairs of socks, pants, or shorts.

Making graphs and then reading them is one way to lay the groundwork for more elaborate data analysis. Going through the process of collecting the data will add to the effectiveness of this activity.

How to Play: Once you find items to graph, set up your graph in a simple format. Write the possible colors across the bottom. Then mark X's on top of each color when you find an item that color. After you have recorded all the colors, count the X's in each category. Talk about the results with your child using terms like "least," "most," "none," and "the same." Continue to graph different items for as long as you and your child have interest in this activity.

12. Predicting Numbers

Objective: To teach your child about predicting events that are more likely, less likely, or equally likely to occur.

About the Game: Use a dice for this activity. If you do not have one, make one with a small block. Place stick-on dots on the sides making one, two, three, four, five, and six dot combinations.

How to Play: Set up a situation for predicting. Together make a prediction and then graph the results. Here are some samples to graph:

• Ones compared to all other numbers. Which will be more? Which will be less?

What are the chances?

- Twos compared to all other numbers. Which will be more? Which will be less?
- Sixes compared to fours. Which will be more? Which will be less?

This hands-on activity will introduce your child to the exciting field of chance and probability.

2

Games for Science

If cognitive development is learning about the world, science is basic to the whole concept. Studying science gives us insight into the world around us. First, the scientific method is a foundation tool. Then the content of science is basic to all of our life's activities. The nature of matter is important to everything we touch and use. Knowledge of energy, force, and motion are at the heart of our mobile society. Earth and space exploration continue to influence life daily. Then here on Earth we work day in and day out to improve the human condition, a study that encompasses all of animal and plant life. Last but not least is the world of technology. While these areas have great complexity, it is valuable to introduce all of these concepts to young children on the simplest levels. They will be experiencing all these aspects of life and need to be made aware during these early years of their lifetime role of caring for themselves and the world around them.

Whereas science of old was explained to children or presented to them through books, science of today is presented in a hands-on manner. For example, telling children that heating water causes it to boil and that making it very cold causes it to freeze is one thing, showing them the processes is another; but having them safely participate in changing the state of water in these two different ways is what really makes the learning take place. Telling children about snow and showing them pictures of it are valuable ways to teach about snow, but seeing it fall and playing in it are the real ways to get to understand it.

"Science" is defined in the *American Heritage Dictionary of the English Language* (p. 1616) as "The observation, identification, description, experimental investigation, and theoretical explanation of phenomena."

The following games have been taken from these areas of study:

Scientific Process—The principles of discovery necessary for scientific investigation, generally involving observation, the formulation of a hypothesis, experimentation, and a conclusion.

Matter—Something that occupies space and can be perceived by one or more senses. This refers to a physical body or a physical substance that has observable or measurable properties.

Energy, Force, and Motion—Energy is the capacity for work or physical change. Force is an aspect of energy that can be described, measured, and predicted. Motion is the movement that results from energy and force.

Earth and Space—Earth is the third planet from the sun and is made up of land, water, an atmosphere of air and inhabited by animals and plants. Space is the universe of which the Earth is a part.

Animals and Plant Life—Animals are living beings with the capacity for mobility and the ability to respond to stimuli; they also have restricted growth and a fixed body structure. Plants are photosynthetic organisms that characteristically produce embryos, contain chloroplasts, have cellulose cell walls, and lack the power of locomotion.

Technology—Technology is the application of science to industrial or commercial objectives.

Scientific Process

1. The Scientific Method

Objective: To teach your child the elements of problem solving related to the scientific method.

About the Game: Use a set of colored three-by-five-inch index cards to set up this game. On one color write "I" and the word "Observation." On a second write "II" and the word "Hypothesis." Use another color for "III" and the word "Experimentation" and a fourth for "IV" and the word "Conclusion." Then take out a group of items. Plastic clothespins are a suggestion. If you do not have clothespins available, here are some other suggested items: a set of blocks, plastic silverware, paper cups, and bottle caps. You may think of other materials.

This is an important problem-solving process. The more experience your child has with it, the more he will get used to it. The idea is for him to be able to apply it to daily life situations now and then in more sophisticated ways in the future.

How to Play: Place the four cards out in order near the group of items. Start with the first card, "Observation," and take turns describing the clothespins. Help your child as much as is needed with his turn. Here are some possible observational terms. There are many.

- Hard
- Light
- Colored

Go on to the next card, "Hypothesis," and think of one hypothesis related to the clothespins. Either you or your child can make the hypothesis. Here are some samples.

- Can stack them.
- Can break them in half.
- Can put them all in a line.

Use the "Experimentation" card and have fun testing your hypothesis.

- Stack them.
- Try to break one in half.
- Put them in a line.

Show the "Conclusion" card and draw a conclusion based on your experimentation.

The scientific method.

Repeat this four-part activity as many times as you and your child continue to enjoy it.

2. *Three Little Plants*

Objective: To teach your child how to do a scientific experiment.

About the Game: Buy three identical plants from a convenient place. Set them up in a place where your child can water them easily.

How to Play: Observe together different aspects of healthy plants. Then talk about plant care and different types of watering. Together make a hypothesis about these three different solutions:

- Water
- Coca-Cola
- Milk

Then begin your experiment by watering each of the plants with one of the solutions. Make an appropriate watering schedule, probably about twice a week. Then watch daily how well each of the plants flourishes and together draw your conclusion about which of the three ways is the best for taking care of these plants. Using this experiment as a model, design other experiments for you and your child using the scientific method.

Matter

3. Paste a Pasta

Objective: To teach your child that you can mix certain materials together to get other materials.

About the Game: Paste is a common material in the life of a child. By going through the process of making it together, you are providing new insight for your child.

How to Play: Put some flour on a paper plate. A quarter cup is a good amount for starting. Then add water slowly. Again, a quarter cup will work well. Use a spoon to mix it until it becomes the consistency of paste. Taking into account your child's age and experience, guide him to participate as much as possible. Then go ahead and set up a pasting activity. Have several pieces of colored paper ready and some pasta pieces, any shape is fine. You can even use spaghetti or lasagna noodles that you break apart into smaller pieces.

Have fun pasting. Take turns being the one who puts the paste on the paper and the one who puts the pasta on the areas with paste on them. As you apply paste to the paper, use your index finger; dip it into the paste, and then on the paper. Show your child how to do the same thing. Then as you place each piece of pasta on a pasted spot, show your child how to do that as well. Have fun designing different papers in different ways.

4. Sink or Float

Objective: To teach your child about the qualities of different objects.

About the Game: Water play is great fun for your child. You can do it in many ways. It can be as elaborate as in a bathtub or small pool, or it can be as simple as in a small sink or wash-basin. Feel free to set one up to your convenience.

How to Play: Collect small play or household items and put them out near your water-play area. Take turns picking an item. Before you place it in the water, say one of these two sentences, "I think this will float." "I think this will not float." Being right or wrong about what you think is not important. The fun will be in seeing what actually happens. Here are some suggested items. You may have others that you would like to use.

- Small ball
- Cotton ball
- Penny
- Drink stirrer
- Spoon
- Sponge
- Soap
- Pencil
- Block
- Toy car

Energy, Force, and Motion

5. Make Your Own Bubbles

Objective: To teach your child that it takes energy and force to set something in motion.

About the Game: Being able to participate in making the solution for blowing the bubbles enhances the actual experience of blowing them.

How to Play: Use the Dawn brand of dishwasher soap. Fill a measuring cup with a half-cup of Dawn. Then add two tablespoons of water. Then mix the solution. Depending on the age of your child, have him do as much of this process on his own as possible. Use the head of children's plastic scissors as the dipping stick into the bubbles solution. Take turns with your child dipping the scissors in the solution and blowing the bubbles. As you or your child blow, hold the scissors sideways over the measuring cup so that the excess liquid will drip back into the cup.

6. Ball Roll

Objective: To teach your child that increasing the incline of a flat surface makes a ball roll faster.

About the Game: Playing with a ball delights just about any child. First rolling and then throwing it bring great fun. Because it never does the same thing twice, it holds an exciting intrigue. Roll it harder, and it will go further. Throw it with more force, and it will go faster.

How to Play: Take a few books down off of a shelf. Make sure one of them is long and wide, about eight and a half by eleven inches in size. Start with a small stack of two books and the big one set up as a ramp. Then take turns rolling the ball down the ramp. Continue to add one book at a time and continue to take turns rolling the ball down the ramp. You and your child can both enjoy watching the ball roll faster and faster each time you increase the angle of the incline. Continue having fun with the ball in any way you and your child wish.

Earth and Space

7. Nature and Not

Objective: To teach your child the difference between natural and man-made products.

About the Game: Outdoor play is appealing to any child.

How to Play: Go outside with your child. Anywhere you choose to play is fine. It could be a nearby place like your own

Rolling the ball.

backyard, the grounds where you live, or a local park; or it could be a place that is further away like somewhere on a trip, at the beach, or outside a friend's house. Take turns finding something outdoors. It could be a product of nature like a stone, twig, or some grass; or it could be a man-made product like hardtop on a driveway, cement on a sidewalk, or a rubber ball or some other playground equipment. As you choose an item, say, "I found a ____. It is from nature." Or "I found a ____. It is man-made." Help your child as much as is necessary in identifying the object as being from nature or man-made.

8. The Solar System

Objective: To teach your child information and awareness about the solar system.

I found a tree. It is from nature.

About the Game: Basic understanding about the Earth and outer space is quite technical. However, providing your child with as much information about it as he can understand is beneficial. Here are some simple basic facts:

- There are nine planets that rotate about the Sun.
- Earth is the third planet from the Sun.
- The order of the planets from the Sun is Mercury, Venus, Earth, Mars, Jupiter, Saturn, Uranus, Neptune, and Pluto.
- The Moon is made of rock and is lit up by the Sun.

- Stars are gigantic balls of hot, shining gasses, trillions and trillions of miles away.
- The Sun is a star, a gigantic ball of hot, shining gases.
- The Sun is the closest star to Earth at 93 million miles away.
- The Sun is smaller than many other stars, but it looks bigger because it is closer to Earth.

How to Play: Take twelve index cards, three-by-five or four-by-six inches. On nine of them draw each of the planets—Mercury, Venus, Earth, Mars, Jupiter, Saturn, Uranus, Neptune, and Pluto. On each of the other three draw the Sun, Moon, and a group of stars. Draw Saturn large with its famous prominent rings around it, and draw Jupiter and Uranus large with thinner rings around them. Make Jupiter the biggest planet but smaller than the Sun. Color Mars red and make Venus the same size as Earth. Make Mercury and Pluto small planets and Neptune bigger than Earth and Venus. Write the corresponding names on another set of twelve cards. Make a second set of drawings of the planets, sun, moon, and stars cards and a second set of the corresponding name cards. Then set up twenty-four cards like a game of concentration. Start with matching pictures to pictures. Then match names to names. Then when your child is ready, do pictures to names.

These cards, which are easy to make, can provide many enjoyable and educational experiences. Having the small amount of reference material available in this activity, you can tell your child as much or as little as you think will be beneficial. You can also add in this useful phrase for remembering the planets in order away from the sun: Many Very Eager Men Just Stay Up Nights Playing.

Animals and Plant Life

9. The Breath of Life

Objective: To teach your child awareness of breathing and its vital connection to life.

About the Game: The gift of life is magnificent. Breathing is the major automatic process that keeps us alive. Without air to breathe we cannot live. This is an opportunity to focus on breathing and also on air that is hard to see and feel. The two breathing activities will be healthful, and the one for air will be insightful. Get two balloons.

How to Play: This is a three-part activity:

1. Stand opposite each other and follow a nice breathing rhythm together. You might want to get it going by repeatedly saying, "Breathe in and breathe out." Explain to your child to breathe in through his nose and then out through his mouth. Tell him to hold his hand in front of his mouth and feel the air as he breathes out. You can even modify the phrase to "Oxygen in, carbon dioxide out." Next you can enrich the breathing activity by lifting your hands up to breathe in and lowering them down to breathe out.
2. Lie down next to each other and start up the same breathing pattern. You can say the same phrases as above to start off the breathing in this new position. After you and your child are used to the new position, you should both close your eyes. Now switch your guidance phrase to "Concentrate on your breathing." Try to set up a relaxing pattern of breathing in and out and concentrating on the breathing.

3. Each of you take a balloon and try to blow it up. It is likely that you will both enjoy seeing the air fill out the balloon and also being able to feel it as it becomes contained in the balloon. Either tie the end to keep the air in the balloon or loosen your grip on the end and watch the air go slowly out.

10. Animals and Plants

Objective: To teach your child the difference between alive and not alive, and then to further refine the concept to animals and plants.

About the Game: Take out a colorful magazine or two.

How to Play: Start with the cover and then turn the pages one by one. On each page take turns identifying something alive. If there is nothing alive on your page, keep turning the pages until you get to one with one or more things that are alive. When you find something, say, "Alive—animal. Alive—plant. Alive—person" (you can explain that a person is an animal). Depending on the age and experience of your child, you can name the particular kind of animal or plant. Your activity then might develop into something like "Alive—animal—dog. Alive—plant—roses."

Use this activity to give your child as much information as you want about living things. As you come across Muppets, dolls, and other toys, you can have some interesting conversations. Pictures of crackers in the shape of fish, cooked chicken, and stuffed animals dressed up to ski are examples of pictures you might see that may provide the basis for much interesting conversation.

Technology

11. A Technology Hunt

Objective: To teach your child as much as you would like about technology and how it works.

About the Game: In years past, scientists have predicted the push-button society of today. Now it is here, and we all live it. The important part of this activity is giving your child an awareness of what a large role technology plays in millennium life.

How to Play: Take your child from room to room in your house and find as many examples of technology as you can. As you find each item, allow your child to push some buttons to make something happen. Explain as much as you can about the technology behind each piece of equipment. Tell about each item as simply or with as much complexity as you like. Here are some examples.

Telephone: A telephone takes the sound of your voice and converts it into a form that can make it travel a faraway distance to a new location. A telephone at the new location receives the sounds and converts them from sound waves to voice signals that can be heard and understood. The waves used to go through wires. Now they go through wires, underground cables, and overhead satellites.

Radio: A radio is the receiver of audible signals that are encoded in electromagnetic waves. It requires a complex set of equipment to send the sounds in such a way that you can hear them. Different buttons on the radio allow you to receive different signals.

Computer E-mail.

The explanations can be brief and at the level that you understand them.

12. Computer Time

Objective: To teach your child about the computer.

About the Game: A computer is a high-speed, electronic machine that processes information in an enormous number of ways. One thing it can do is send messages.

How to Play: Find an available computer. Teach your child to send a simple E-mail message to a friend or relative. Help as much or as little as is necessary. When your child gets a response, guide your child as he reads it. As with writing the message, help as much or as little as is necessary.

3

Games for Social Studies

Although for many the term "social studies" might conjure up something dull, this area of study has the potential to be more interesting to humankind than almost any other subject. If mathematics is so intriguing and if science is so enlightening, how could this be so? It is because social studies is about humanity . . . how we function on our own in terms of *psychology* and how we function in groups in terms of *sociology*. It also includes how we were in years past as a way of learning about better ways to be in the future, the aspect we call *history*. Then there is the newest application of this field, which we call *relationship skills training*, and the newest subject area that has seeped into our school system as a whole, *character development*.

Self-awareness and self-esteem are at the heart of this subject area. It actually becomes more focused than that. It is about love. Parents are the first ones to feel this for their newborn. They then take it in its purist state and deliver it to their baby. If society were simpler, the baby would continue to receive the purity of this love over the first five years, the foundation years responsible for setting up the child success-fully for the rest of his life. However, society is not simple, and with child care and all the other socioeconomic problems that enter the picture, young children do not receive the full quality of this pure tender loving care so necessary to their optimal development.

The term "social" is defined in the *American Heritage Dictio-nary of the English Language* (p. 1710) as "Living together in communities."

The following games have been taken from these areas of study:

Psychology—The science that deals with an individual, focusing on mental, emotional, and behavioral proc-esses. It includes the development of self-awareness and self-esteem.

Sociology—The study of human social behavior, espe-cially organizations and institutions. It starts with the family, then extends to community, and then expands to various other social units of society.

History—A chronological record of events of a person, family, community, or society.

Relationships—Connections existing between people.

Character Development—Bringing to fulfillment moral or ethical strength.

Psychology

1. Me Box

Objective: To teach your child a sense of self-awareness and self-esteem.

About the Game: Build this together with your child. As you both contribute items, you will both add insights into getting at the essence of your child's uniqueness.

How to Play: Select a container for your child's Me Box. It doesn't have to be a box. It can be a grocery bag, shopping bag, a shoebox, or some other bag, lunch box, or backpack that you both identify with your child. Then have fun with your child collecting five to ten items to go in that container that are representative of your child.

2. Educational Display

Objective: To teach your child that the work he does in school or at home is valued.

About the Game: It has become customary in our society to hang a child's work on the family refrigerator. This practice provides for a child a small area in which to display the important work he does in a preschool, child care, or home setting. This game provides a large area for hanging this kind of work.

How to Play: Set up a small decorator fishnet display on a wall. You can use a wall in your child's room, a hallway, or family

Me box.

room. Place two hooks on the wall on which to hang the net. You can use suction hooks or stick-on hooks, whichever you think will work better for your situation. If you cannot find a fishnet, often available in a local party supply store, you can also use one or more six-, seven-, and eight-foot pieces of yarn or string hung in loops from the hooks. Use a set of ten to twenty plastic clothespins to hang up your child's work.

The important part of this game begins as soon as the work is up. Whenever you pass it by, comment on it . . . the quality, color, style, or other form of uniqueness. This acknowledgment is what will help to build for your child his self-worth, importance, value, and capability. It will give you a concrete way of expressing both appreciation and respect for what he has done.

Sociology

3. My Family Collage

Objective: To teach your child that he is an important part of a family unit.

About the Game: Use a colored file folder for this project. A folder adds an element of surprise to the game. Whenever you play with your collage, your child will always have the fun of surprise as he opens the folder to find out what is inside.

How to Play: With a marker write "My Family" on the front of the file folder. Use the inside to place photos of people in your child's family. Use double-sided tape to attach each photo to the opened folder. Place the tape on the back of each photo and have your child place the photos in a collage-like fashion anywhere in the folder. As more people or pets enter the family, or as you get more pictures of other family members, have your child place them in the collage folder.

4. My Friends

Objective: To teach your child an awareness of the wonderful people who are in his life.

About the Game: Naming the different people whom your child knows will help him realize how many different people affect him in positive ways.

How to Play: Take a set of three-by-five-inch index cards. Ask your child to name adults and children with whom he spends time on a regular basis. Write each name on a separate card. Then collect these cards. You can write adult names in one color and child names in another. This set of cards will show your child the size and depth of his social circle. Each time you play, you can add new people to the cards and take away any who no longer interact with your child. If you have matching photos and want to add them to the backs of the cards with double-sided tape, that would enhance the activity.

History

5. When I Was Your Age . . .

Objective: To teach your child about what it was like for you when you were his age.

About the Game: Your child will enjoy hearing about what life was like for you when you were a child. As you share this information, you and your child will become closer, and you will enrich your relationship.

How to Play: Sit with your child in a favorite spot. A soft couch is fine, a comfortable bed, or a big easy chair are suggestions. Tell your child something interesting about your childhood. It could be something your mother used to say to you all the time. It could be what she gave you to eat. It could be about bedtime, toys, or your friends. Share as much as you will enjoy. Then switch to questions. Say, "Ask me a question, and I will be happy to answer it." Have fun as you answer your child's questions.

A timeline for Amanda.

6. Time Line

Objective: To teach your child about his life, what has happened so far, and the kind things to strive for in the future.

About the Game: A timeline will give your child a visual picture of his life. The years he has lived will become clearer and more meaningful. Discussing the years to come will provide a vision of the future. As they say, "It is hard to get there unless you know where you are going."

How to Play: Using index cards, any size, make a timeline for your child starting with his year of birth; have a card for each year after his birth to the present. As you point to each year, tell your child something significant about his life that happened in that year.

Once you finish talking about the years, you can go on and talk about things to come. You can make cards for different years ahead and make some predictions about those years. It is fine to take the conversation all the way up to adulthood and to have a conversation about the kind of adult you and he envision he will become.

Relationships

7. Play and Say

Objective: To teach your child a poem that is a vehicle for people getting to know each other.

About the Game: The first two lines are for participation. The next five are for listening. The last part is for pleasant interaction.

Hello, what is your name?
How old are you?
Glad to meet you.
Yes, it's true.
Let's play a game that's fun to do.
Listen to the words I choose,
And tell me what it is you use.
What do you drink from?
What do you eat with?
What is the food on?
What do you like to eat?
What do you like to drink?

Glad to meet you.

What do you like to play?
What do you like to say?

How to Play: Start by asking the first question. Wait for an answer. Then ask the second question following the same procedure. When you start line three, put out your hand for a handshake and start the "Glad to meet you" section of the poem.

The last part is for developing verbal expression. After much repetition, you and your child will get to know this poem like an old friend. You will be able to take it with you from memory wherever you go. It can be a diversion in a car ride, at the park, or in any place of your choice.

8. Row, Row, Row Your Boat

Objective: To teach your child the joy of participating in a shared activity.

About the Game: Singing together adds to shared time together. In addition, adding movement to the activity increases its effectiveness.

How to Play: Sit opposite your child on the floor, preferably on a nice soft rug. Place your heels against each other and join hands. Then rock back and forth to the tune of "Row, Row, Row Your Boat." Pull lightly on your child's hands, and encourage him to develop strength by pulling a little harder on yours.

Character Development

9. Story of the Day

Objective: To teach your child about honesty and integrity through exercising the memory.

About the Game: Because the most interesting story a child could hear is one about himself and because information for this kind of story is readily available, a story about your child's own experiences during the day is fun and easy to tell. Bedtime is an excellent time for this activity. It is a nice way to end the day because it recaps for your child the events of the day. You can weave the thread of the story and have your child fill in details.

How to Play: Begin the story in the same way each time. "Once upon a time" is the traditional story opener, but you can make up others like "This is the story of the day of (Name)" or "On (date), (Name) woke up, saw the daylight, and hugged his mom and dad." You can also repeat in this story the child's address, phone number, birthday, and any other facts you would like him to learn. Then go on to tell the events of the day. Your child can participate in the story by providing information about what actually happened. As your child goes through the events of the day, you can stop and discuss any particular event that lends itself to teaching a lesson of honesty and integrity.

10. Please and Thank You

Objective: To teach your child to say, "Please" and "Thank you."

About the Game: The real way to get your child to say "Please" and "Thank you" is to say, "Please" and "Thank you" to your child.

How to Play: Set up a snack time for you and your child. Put out two place settings. Then in the middle of the table put a pitcher of juice, some crackers, and a spread of your choice like peanut butter, cream cheese, or humus. Different cultures will have a preference for different items.

Begin the conversation with, "Please pass the . . . ." Then say, "Thank you." Then ask your child what he wants. If it is not yet natural, teach your child to say, "Please pass the . . . ." Have fun taking turns asking for different items set out on the table. Enjoy your snack together.

11. I Can . . .

Objective: To teach your child that he is capable by helping him gain awareness of the many things he can do.

About the Game: If a child is aware of what he can do, he will have a positive feeling about himself. If he feels positive about himself, he will treat himself kindly. If he treats himself kindly, he is likely in turn to treat others kindly. So many children have a bad feeling about themselves. Often this feeling comes from negative messages: "You can't do that." "Don't do that." "Stop it." "Put that away."

How to Play: Take turns saying and showing something that you can do. Here are some examples:

1. I can jump five times.
2. I can spell my name.
3. I can count to ten.
4. I can sit in a chair.
5. I can open a door.
6. I can find my slippers.
7. I can touch my toes.
8. I can clap my hands.
9. I can read a book.
10. I can color a picture.

12. I Like . . .

Objective: To teach your child to look for good in life in general and to be able to express it as well.

About the Game: If a child gains experience in saying things that are positive, he will be more likely to say them in a natural setting. So many children have a negative attitude and are unhappy. They often complain when no one is doing something to specifically entertain them. They miss out on enjoying simple everyday activities.

I like . . .

How to Play: Take turns saying what you like to do. Use simple sentences starting with the words, "I like." Here are some examples:

1. I like to look through photo albums.
2. I like to pour from pitchers.
3. I like to walk on the street.
4. I like to play ball.

5. I like looking at the blue sky and trees.
6. I like holding your hand.
7. I like singing a song.
8. I like running.
9. I like going to sleep at night.
10. I like eating a roast beef sandwich.

PART TWO

Motor Development

Motor development refers to muscular movement. There are two kinds of muscular movement—gross motor and fine motor. Gross-motor development starts with such movements as lifting the head and chest while lying on the stomach and ends with milestones like learning to ride a two-wheeled bike, skating, and doing somersaults. There is a definite order to gross-motor movements, and you will find many charts that list this order. Fine-motor development takes place over time and is related to the pincer grasp (thumb and forefinger dexterity), wrist control, and general manipulative skills in the hand with the fingers. There is a progression too, but it is more vague. It eventually will show up as writing, drawing, painting, cutting, and related skills.

Midline movements are another aspect of motor development. Crossing the midline of the body is an important skill for learning. Being able to easily reach an object with your right hand on the left side of your body and with your left hand on the right side of your body is an important prerequisite for reading and writing. You must be able to cross the midline of your body with your eyes in order to learn to read, and you must be able to cross it with your hands in order to be able to learn to write. Often children who are delayed in showing hand preference need practice in this area. Those children who find it difficult to take things on the right side with their left hand and on the left side with their right hand need practice in using their hands to cross the midline of their bodies.

While the benchmarks of motor development happen naturally, they are dependent on an optimal environment. They can be delayed by a poor environment and advanced by a rich one. As a parent, you have the opportunity to play with your child in such a way that you can enhance gross-motor, fine-motor, and midline movements. While your child has an inborn drive to move and a directive spirit of curiosity, you will have the ideas and materials to enrich the process.

Motor activities contribute to learning in another way. They provide stimulation to the brain. Rocking and swinging movements are very important. They give off impulses that are related to maintaining balance in the brain. All movements send messages to the brain about those movements. Although our culture has a way of separating motor development from learning and brain development, in reality the two are intricately connected. The brain is totally responsible for all movement, and all movements are recorded in the brain.

A good example of the impact of gross-motor development is learning to hit a ball with a bat. The brain directs you through all the movements. When you swing, your movements are recorded in your brain. They then influence you for the next time. How wonderful it is to get into proper motor-skill habits and how difficult it is to change learned patterns.

A good example of the power of fine-motor development is learning to hold a pencil correctly. How wonderful it is to learn to hold it in the right position, evenly balanced between the thumb, forefinger, and middle finger, and how difficult it is to break an old pattern and learn to hold it correctly after that.

There are many activities in normal development that relate to midline skills. Crawling, which usually starts somewhere between six and nine months, practices a cross-patterning movement that is a natural part of this process. Tricycle and then bicycle riding also develops a body balance that works on this same midline development.

This connection between the brain and motor skills is continually at work and is directly related to the growing brain. There is rapid brain growth from birth through five years of age, and it slows down by about age six. It becomes quite slow between ages six and eight and comes almost to a stop between ages eight and ten. The brain continues to grow and learn forever but never again as fast and as well as it does in the early years. It grows fastest and learns the most from birth and keeps slowing down after that.

This is the time to turn your growing child's energy into activities of fun and frolic. Through action games you give your child an exciting venue for developing in an optimal way. Here are the building blocks on which you can design motor activities:

Gross Motor

- Hopping, jumping, skipping, and galloping.
- Walking upstairs without holding a rail.
- Learning to ride a two-wheeled bike.
- Learning to skate.
- Learning to do somersaults, cartwheels, and crabwalks.

Fine Motor

- Cutting and pasting.
- Tying a knot.

- Stringing large beads.
- Scribbling and drawing.
- Cutting on a line with scissors.
- Writing numbers up to ten.
- Printing name.
- Fastening, buckling, and tying.
- Catching a ball.
- Coloring within lines.
- Doing puzzles.

Midline

- Having arms spread out and then crossing them.
- Arm stretches from the right side to the left and vice versa.
- Arm stretches to opposite toes.
- Jumping jacks.

The categories for this topic are gross motor, fine motor, and midline. These three areas cover all basic movements. Motor movements develop from the inside out and from the top down. For gross-motor movements, you will be able to set up games that provide aerobic exercises, stretching exercises, muscle building, traditional play, and sports. For fine-motor development, you will be able to introduce games with manipulatives, wrist strengthening, the pincer grasp, scribbling and drawing, and building with many different kinds of blocks. For midline there will be games that cross the midline and others that meet at the midline. All of these game activities will always take place within the process of growth. More and more experience with them will produce finer and finer results.

4

Games for
Gross-Motor Development

One of the best things you can do for a young child is take him to a playground. Besides the playtime and physical exercise time you know you are providing, you are actually giving your child the opportunity to grow in other ways as well.

Each piece of equipment moves or helps your child move through space in a way important for proper developmental growth. Swings move your child back and forth, merry-go-rounds around, slides up and down, and jungle gyms in all directions.

There are also many movement activities you can do at home, some inside and some outside. Some are exercises, and some lay the foundation for more advanced exercises. Some are games and sports, and some lay the foundation for later games and sports. Some refine general body coordination, and some build muscles. All develop concentration that is so valuable to all future endeavors.

1. Warm Up, Cool Down

Objective: To teach your child how to do aerobic activity.

About the Game: Running, jumping, hopping, skipping, and galloping are all activities your child will enjoy. As he participates he will be exercising his heart and his whole circulatory system. Appropriate exercise will provide a slow start, rapid activity, and then a slow ending.

How to Play: Either outside or inside find a large area where your child can move around in an active way. Select an agreed-upon activity from this list—running, jumping, hopping, skipping, and galloping. Then take turns giving the directions. Let your child go first. Here is an example: Select running. Rotate the directions in this way—slow, fast, slow—so that your child will be getting genuine exercise. Then you take your turn and have your child give you the directions. Repeat this game with other selections from the activity list.

2. Exercise Stations

Objective: To teach your child how to do aerobic exercise in a small space.

About the Game: There are several active movements that can be done in place. Here are three popular ones: running,

Here I go!

jumping, and jumping jacks. You may think of others like hopping, if that is something your child particularly likes to do.

How to Play: Take three sheets of copy paper and write with a marker in large clear letters a different movement on each piece of paper. Place each paper in a different corner of the room. Take turns doing what it says on each piece of paper. Count to ten as you and your child do the actions. Then move to a different sheet of paper. Again, count to ten as you and your child each do the actions. Continue play as long as you both keep your interest in the game.

3. Moving and Dancing to the Music

Objective: To teach your child to get exercise and fun from music.

About the Game: Dance music is readily available on the radio.

How to Play: Turn the radio on to music with a good beat. Then have fun dancing. Feel free to copy each other, do different steps, or enjoy each other as dance partners.

4. The X-ercise

Objective: To teach your child about the X in his body and the idea of working on that concept.

About the Game: With hands stretched high and wide overhead and legs out to shoulder width, your body is like an X. There are many stretching exercises that reinforce this natural shape.

   Implicit in this game is the opportunity to cross the midline of the body. This is beneficial for helping the left and right sides of the brain to work together. In addition, it is reinforcing for the reading and writing processes.

How to Play: Take the X position opposite your child. Show him how to do it as well. Then begin stretches that foster this shape. With outstretched arms, rotate touching your left foot with your right hand and your right foot with your left hand. You can also do reaches at your waist with arms high from left to right and from right to left. Arm circles are good too.

5. Pillow Pulls

Objective: To teach your child to do body stretches.

About the Game: A simple pillow from a couch or bed can be used for this activity.

How to Play: Take two pillows, one for you and one for your child, and place each one on the floor. Each of you lie on your pillows opposite the other. Then begin your stretches. You give the directions and try to encourage your child to follow your directions. Here are some ideas:

- Stretch your arms and your legs up.
- Stretch your right arm and your left leg up.
- Stretch your left arm and your right leg up.
- Stretch your head up.
- Stretch your whole body out as long as it can be.
- Point and then flex your feet.
- Circle your feet first a few times one way and then a few times the other way.

6. Child Olympics

Objective: To teach your child different movements.

About the Game: Use an exercise mat or a carpeted area for this activity.

How to Play: Set up a performance area. Explain that you will take turns doing various stunts. If you like doing any of the

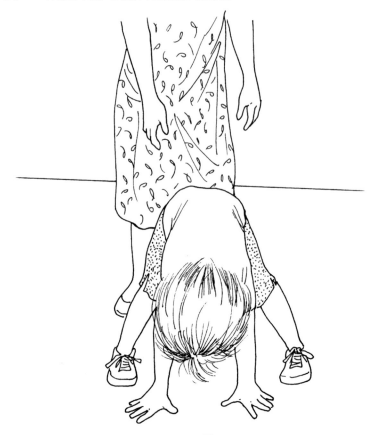

I can roll over.

stunts, take your turn. If not, just guide your child through different positions. If you feel you cannot safely spot your child as he does the movements, please do not do them. Either get help from a friend or relative or skip the activity altogether. Here are some suggested age-appropriate tumbles:

- Somersaults
- Cartwheels
- Headstands
- Crabwalks

7. Sit-ups and Push-ups

Objective: To teach your child how to strengthen important muscle groups.

About the Game: Basic sit-ups and push-ups and all their variations provide excellent muscle-strengthening activities.

How to Play: Start with sit-ups. Lie down on the floor with your child and model the crunch position. Suggest he clasp his hands behind his head for support, bend his knees, and keep his feet flat on the floor. You can also try to teach him to breathe out and tighten his stomach muscles each time he lifts his shoulders and back to come up halfway. See how many he can comfortably do. Anywhere between 5 and 12 is a good starting number. Then take your turn. Switch back and forth as you play. Each time try to add one more crunch sit-up to the number you had done before. Three sets are recommended for this activity.

Push-ups provide an excellent muscle-building activity. The suggested position is with your two hands and your knees touching the floor. As with the sit-up activity, take your turns separately so that you can count for and with each other. Also, as with the sit-ups, try to increase your number each time each of you takes your turn.

8. Hokey Pokey

Objective: To teach your child to play an enjoyable activity that has many different kinds of movements.

About the Game: This game provides a wonderful way to teach or reinforce the concepts of left and right. It is also valuable for teaching or reinforcing the direction of "clockwise." Consistently going from left to right and moving in the clockwise direction establishes an order for movement and provides grounding for developing a sense of position in space.

How to Play: Stand opposite each other and play this well-known game. Here is a recommended order for body parts to place in the center between the two of you:

- Left hand, right hand
- Left foot, right foot
- Head
- Whole self

When you "do the hokey pokey," you can be creative about this movement. When you "turn yourself about," you and your child should turn in the clockwise direction.

9. Mother, or Father, May I

Objective: To teach your child an activity for interesting and enjoyable movements.

About the Game: Following directions is a side benefit that comes with this movement activity.

How to Play: Take turns being "Mother or Father." You can start. Give your child interesting and fun directions to follow. After you give each direction, your child says, "May I?" Then you have the option to say, "Yes, you may" or "No, you may not." If you say, "Yes, you may," your child can go ahead and follow the direction. If you say, "No, you may not," you can

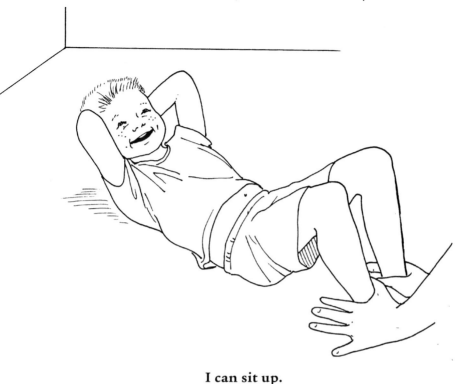

I can sit up.

give another direction. With just the two of you, you can continue play as long as you both want to and change roles as often as you both want to as well. When play involves more people, the strategy changes a little. The caller starts out far away from the players. Eventually the players get closer, and one of them is able to tag the caller. The one who tags first then becomes the caller.

10. Simon Says

Objective: To teach your child another activity for interesting and enjoyable movements.

About the Game: Following directions is a side benefit that also comes with this movement activity.

How to Play: Take turns being "Simon." You can start. Give your child interesting and fun directions to follow. Start each direction with the words, "Simon says." Explain to your child that when you say "Simon says" it is okay for him to follow the direction. Then explain that when you do not say "Simon says" it is not okay to follow the direction. Have fun with the whole idea of saying and not saying "Simon says." With just the two of you, you can continue play as long as you both want to and change roles as often as you both want to. When play involves more people, the strategy changes a little. If a player follows the direction without having "Simon says" in front of the direction, he is out. With a group of players, the last one to be out will be Simon for the next round.

11. Bowling

Objective: To teach your child eye-hand coordination while laying the foundation for learning to bowl.

About the Game: Empty 12-ounce or 18-ounce plastic water bottles make excellent bowling pins for this game. You will need ten altogether.

How to Play: Set up the empty bottles in one part of the room. Use a rubber ball about ten inches in diameter or a small beach ball. Take turns trying to knock over the bottles with the ball. You should each stand behind the pins when it is not your turn to be able to roll the ball back to the player who is taking

Tennis anyone!

his turn. While there are two tries per player in regular bowling, you can both take as many tries as you need to get them all down. There is no score keeping, just the fun of knocking down the pins.

12. Tennis

Objective: To teach your child eye-hand coordination while laying the foundation for learning to play tennis.

About the Game: Give your child a racquetball racquet. It is a good size and weight for teaching your child beginning tennis.

How to Play: Show your child how to hold the racquet. At different ages, because of varying strength, children will be holding it in different ways. Strive for as close to proper form as possible and focus on telling your child to watch the ball. Then throw a tennis ball or a light sponge ball toward your child's racquet and give your child the best directions you know for how to hit the ball. Help as much or as little as is necessary. Be supportive as you teach. Remember to focus on what to do and talk as little as possible about what not to do.

5

Games for
Fine-Motor Development

There are three major areas of muscle development that need to be worked for fine-motor development—fingers and the hand as they manipulate objects, the forefinger and thumb as they work together in a pincer grasp, and the wrist. Throughout your child's day, he will face many opportunities to exercise in all of those areas. These three areas will act as preparation for writing and drawing. Practice in all areas will help to develop the all-important ability of eye-hand coordination.

Gross-motor development is basic to fine-motor development. The principle is similar to that of a tree's growth. The trunk and root system must be healthy and strong for the branches, stems, and leaves to thrive. Therefore, general body exercise should be kept up along with all the fine-motor experiences.

Many playgrounds have large sand areas for tactile stimulation as well as fine-motor and creativity development. Activities in the sandbox build eye-hand coordination and concentration.

Manipulative

1. Play Dough, Clay, or Putty

Objective: To teach your child how to develop manipulative skills while expanding his creativity.

About the Game: There is a progression of play dough and clay activities that may be followed when this medium is introduced—touching and feeling it for familiarity, rolling into a ball, patting the ball into a pancake, making the pancake into a happy face, and then rolling out the pancake into snakes to coil for building into pottery type figures. This whole series provides stimulation for all the muscles in the fingers and hands. Whether you are using store-bought or homemade play dough, be sure to store it in plastic containers with lids or Ziploc bags so that it will not dry out.

If you are using clay, choose Plasticine that can be left uncovered and still not dry out. Most toy stores or discount stores carry it. In addition, tongue depressors and Popsicle sticks can be used like sculptor's tools.

If you are looking for putty, you will probably have to go to a medical supply store. Most of them sell a product called Theraputty. It comes in four colors—yellow, red, green, and blue. Yellow and red are the softest and are the colors recommended for children. These are nontoxic putty substances that are sold

Putty in your hands.

for stroke patients to build up the dexterity in their hands. For children they provide a safe, convenient, and enjoyable manipulative experience. A good idea is to buy two of these that match. With one for yourself and one for your child, you have an activity you can share together. It is even recommended as a telephone toy. You can both use it together when you are on the telephone. For this time when you have to take your attention away from your child, you and he can still have a shared, enjoyable experience.

How to Play: Each of you take a piece of play dough, clay, or putty the same size. You demonstrate the project with your piece and ask him to try to make what you are making. Go through the progression listed above. From those basics you can make many things—snowmen, people, animals, pottery, and more. You can also make letters out of the snakes. It is often fun to make a letter and cover it up with a washcloth. Then ask your child to feel under the washcloth to try to figure out what the letter is. Your child can also make a letter to hide under the washcloth for you to identify.

2. The Last Straw

Objective: To teach your child manipulative skills while experiencing the concept of ten.

About the Game: Regular drinking straws work best for this game. If straws are not available, you can use a group of ten pencils.

How to Play: Stand opposite each other and get ready to pass a group of ten straws in a clockwise direction. Start by holding all ten in your right hand. Then pass them one at a time to your left hand. Then pass them one at a time to your child's right hand opposite your left hand. Ask your child to pass the straws one at a time to his own left hand. Then ask him to pass them one at a time to your right hand. Keep passing the straws one at a time around in this clockwise direction.

Each time you pass them, try to do it faster and faster. In addition, you can count the straws as you pass each one. If one drops as you play, pick it right up. That will be part of the play. For each turn you always want to make sure you have passed the last straw.

3. Where is Thumbkin?

Objective: To teach your child how to do finger exercises while singing a song.

About the Game: This is an age-old children's song passed down from generation to generation that provides finger exercises. The more practice your child has with this song, the better he will be able to do the finger movements.

How to Play: Sit opposite your child and do the singing and motions of the song together. Help him as much as is necessary to do the proper finger movements on each hand. Here are the words and the corresponding finger motions.

Words	Actions
Where is thumbkin?	Hold up left thumb.
Where is thumbkin?	Hold up right thumb.
Here I am.	Move left thumb.
Here I am.	Move right thumb.
How are you today, sir?	Move left thumb.
Very well I thank you.	Move right thumb.
Run away.	Move left hand behind back.
Run away.	Move right hand behind back.

Repeat the verse four more times, substituting a different finger each time. The index finger is traditionally called "pointer"; the middle finger, "tall man"; the ring finger, "ring man"; and the small outside finger, "pinky."

4. Building Toys

Objective: To teach your child how to build with different kinds of building sets.

About the Game: Any of the building sets available like Lego, blocks, Bristle Blocks, Tinkertoys, Lincoln Logs, and more are good for this activity. If they come with a booklet showing sample structures, save it. The idea behind this activity is to try to build something similar to something you can see. If there is no booklet, or if those pictures in the booklet look too difficult, make a simpler structure as a model. You might also have a bottle-cap collection for building. For those, you could also draw a model structure. Tangrams, a set of eight pieces cut from a square that can be formed into many different shapes, is another good alternative. A set comes with a booklet showing different pictures you can make. It is available at most specialty educational toy stores.

How to Play: Show the picture or the model to your child. Ask him to try to build one the same. Help as little or as much as is necessary. This kind of activity also helps to develop map-reading skills.

Pincer Grasp

5. Tearing and Pasting Paper

Objective: To teach your child how to tear small pieces of paper.

About the Game: Construction paper is good for tearing. White copy paper is good for the background. Simple paste is easy to apply with your forefinger.

How to Play: Show your child how to tear paper into small pieces with his thumb and forefinger. When all the tearing is done, draw your child's initials in thick outlines on the white paper. Then show your child how to spread paste all over the space of the letters. Then show him how to fill the whole pasted area with the torn pieces of construction paper. You can either take turns putting on the mosaic pieces, or you can make your own mosaic with your initials.

6. Button Practice

Objective: To teach your child to develop his pincer grasp while doing an interesting activity.

About the Game: You can use any large piece of clothing that has buttons on it that are of the appropriate size for your child to button and unbutton. A shirt of yours or of an older brother or sister and, a jacket, sweater, or robe of his are other possibilities.

How to Play: Help him put the garment on, crossing one arm into the sleeve and then the other. Find a button in the easiest position and ask him to start with that. Take turns buttoning and then unbuttoning the rest of the garment. He can do all the buttons if he wishes. Help as little or as much as is necessary, showing in a slow way how to hold the button as you push it through the buttonhole.

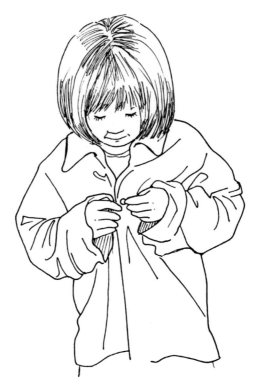

I can button.

7. Itsy Bitsy Spider

Objective: To teach your child dexterity with his forefinger and thumb while learning a traditional nursery song.

About the Game: This is an age-old children's song passed down from generation to generation that provides finger exercises. It also has hand and arm movements. The more practice your child has with this song, the better he will be able to do the motions.

Here are the words and the corresponding finger, hand, and arm motions:

The Itsy Bitsy Spider.

Words	Actions
The itsy, bitsy spider went up the waterspout.	Place thumb to forefinger and forefinger to thumb so that they make a rectangular shape. Keep shifting the bottom thumb and forefinger and raise them slightly as you sing.
Down came the rain and washed the spider out.	Wiggle fingers in a downward motion (like rain). Stretch out arms to the sides.
Out came the sun and dried up all the rain.	Raise hands overhead in a circular position and move from side to side.
And the itsy bitsy spider went up the spout again.	Thumb to forefinger and forefinger to thumb, raising hands as you sing.

How to Play: Sit opposite your child and do the singing and motions of the song together. Help him as much as is necessary to do the suggested movements.

8. Lacing a Shoe

Objective: To teach your child how to lace a shoe.

About the Game: Choose a shoe for this activity that will be fun. An old baby shoe, or a large shoe from an older brother or sister, Mommy, or Daddy will also work well.

How to Play: Take the shoelace out of the shoe. Get the lacing started. Then take turns putting the lace through one hole at a time. If that activity goes well, continue to teach tying the shoelace. Help your child as much as he needs it. Break down the activity into small steps for any part that is difficult for your child.

Look for other shoes around the house that close in other ways. Practice any that have buckles. You might even find some boots with interesting fasteners or zippers or have some fun with any Velcro closings.

Wrist

9. The Tossing Game

Objective: To teach your child to toss effectively.

About the Game: If you have beanbags available, you can use them for this game. If not you can easily make them. One way is with dry beans and small Ziploc bags. Another way is by putting some beans in old socks and then tying the socks tight to seal in the beans. You will also need a small washtub or basin, clean wastepaper basket, plastic crate, large shoebox, or some similar kind of container for the beanbag toss.

How to Play: Place the container a few feet away from your child to his left. Ask him to throw the beanbags into it. Hold the pile of beanbags and hand them to him one at a time. After he has tossed the full collection of beanbags, pick them up and begin the process again. This time place the container directly in front of your child. Again, after he has finished tossing, collect the beanbags, move the container to the right side of your child and begin again. Continue moving the container through the left, center, and right positions. Have fun with this game for as long as you and your child wish to play.

10. Potato Carry

Objective: To teach your child to enjoy a challenging activity.

About the Game: Use a soupspoon or tablespoon and a potato small enough that it will not fall off the spoon easily. If no potatoes are available, use a piece of fruit such as an orange or an apple. If no fruit is available, try an onion or some other object that you may have that is of a similar size and weight.

How to Play: Give your child the potato or equivalent object on the spoon. Check to see that he can balance it well. Then walk a distance away from him, about six feet at first, and then tell him to carry the potato on the spoon back to you. If it is easy for him at this distance, walk farther away the next time. You can do this activity over and over using a greater distance each time. Play a few times in a row and take your turn walking the potato to your child.

11. Lifting Weights

Objective: To teach your child to develop wrist strength and muscle strength at the same time.

About the Game: Make a set of half-pound weights for your child by dividing a pound of sugar into two small Ziploc bags.

How to Play: Show your child how to lift the weights, palm up, into the air. Start with one weight at a time and then switch to two. Count five lifts and then ask him to change hands for five more lifts. After he does it, take your turn. Each time you play, increase the number of lifts by two or three. Continue to play for a few rounds until your child has had enough.

12. Zip

Objective: To teach your child how to zip.

About the Game: You can use any piece of clothing that has a zipper on it large enough that your child will be able to manip-ulate it. A jacket or sweater from any member of the family is a good source.

I can zip!

How to Play: If it is not too large, your child can wear the selected garment. Show him how to hold the material firmly as he
lifts the tab on the zipper up and down. At first you can hook it
at the bottom for him, but later you can show him how to do
that as well. Take turns with him until he has had enough.

6

Games for Midline Development

Crossing the midline is an important stage of development. Almost every activity depends on this ability. With reading you move your eyes across the page. With writing you move your hand across it. In sports you move the bat, racquet, or club across it. It is a basic skill.

Beginning ability to cross the midline starts to develop when a child is a few months old, and it is continually being refined. Hand preference starts to show up at about two years of age, and hand dominance is usually established by about the age of five.

While crossing the midline is the goal for normal development, the process starts with being aligned at the midline. One of the first milestones of motor development is lifting your head. That is something that needs to be done straight up. After that all the other milestones must also be done in a symmetrical position—sitting up, crawling, standing, and more. The next extension is movements that are done to meet at the midline like clapping hands. After that it is important to keep in mind that as you direct your child in the most basic movements and exercises, his body should be midline centered with his head facing forward.

The term "midline" is defined in the *American Heritage Dictionary of the English Language* (p. 1142) as "A medial line, especially the medial line or plane of the body."

The following games have been designed around crossing the midline and meeting at the midline.

Crossing the Midline

1. Cross the Midline

Objective: To teach your child to cross the midline of his body.

About the Game: This game becomes more fun the more you play it. It is a simple task that you can do faster and faster. You can use a small ball for the activity or some other small object.

How to Play: Hold the small ball or other object on the left side of your child's body. Also hold down his left hand so that he must take the object with his right hand. Retrieve the ball or object and place it on the right side of your child's body. Hold down the right hand and ask him to get the object with his left hand. Repeat the activity over and over for several

I got it!

minutes. Expect that you both will have some silly laughs. After he gets the hang of it, he may even want to try this activity with you. Why not!

2. Checkerboard Patterns

Objective: To teach your child to cross the midline of his body with his eyes.

About the Game: Start this game with simple patterns, and then you can progress to harder patterns.

How to Play: With an open checkerboard and checkers in front of you, place a few checkers in squares on your side of the board. Then have your child place checkers in the corresponding squares on his side. Add one to your side and ask him to place a corresponding one on his side. Continue the game as much as you feel is appropriate. Then clear the board and start again. You can also take turns starting. Once each pattern is complete, you can talk about the positions of different checkers with descriptive words like "on the left of," "on the right of," "on top of," "under," "next to," and so on.

3. Follow the Yarn

Objective: To teach your child to cross the midline of his body with his eyes.

About the Game: Use a short piece of yarn or ribbon about nine to twelve inches long. You can also substitute a flashlight for the yarn. The important part of the activity is having your child keep his head straight while moving his eyes.

How to Play: Have your child sit up straight on a chair with his head looking up at you. Then move the yarn slowly across his body from his left side to his right. Ask him to follow it with his eyes. Encourage him to keep his head straight while following the yarn with his eyes.

If you choose to use a flashlight, project the light on a wall in front of your child. Then, as with the yarn, ask him to follow it with his eyes only from left to right.

4. Eye Exercise

Objective: To teach your child how to cross the midline of his body with his eyes.

About the Game: This game is especially helpful to a child who has weak muscles in his eyes. It will help him focus better. At first some children may need extra help keeping their heads still while learning to move just their eyes.

How to Play: With your child sitting opposite you, ask him to look at your face. Then show some of your fingers on the right side of his body and ask him to say how many there are. Ask him to move only his eyes to that side to see, not his head. Take away the fingers on the right side and show some on the left. Again ask him to identify the number of fingers without moving his head. Repeat showing fingers from side to side and asking him to look at them without moving his head. If he wants to, he can try the fingers game with you.

5. Arms Together Side-to-Side

Objective: To teach your child how to cross the midline of his body with his arms.

About the Game: Any object that your child can grasp comfortably can be used. At first you might have to hold your child's head still. Later he may be able to find a spot straight ahead that will help him keep it straight.

How to Play: Place an object like a ball or can in your child's hands and have him clasp it securely in front of him. Then ask him to swing it from side to side across the midline of his body without moving his head. Ask him to look straight ahead at you with his head still and not to look at his waving arms. He should be able to feel the momentum of his arm movements. You can also do the arm swings opposite him to make it more fun. You can both concentrate on moving at your waist. That also makes the process easier. When he gets the hang of it, you can move aside and let him find a spot on a wall ahead to help him keep from moving his head.

6. Jack-in-the-Box

Objective: To teach your child how to cross the midline of his body with his arms.

About the Game: This is a short rhyme, which if acted out properly helps to develop midline awareness. Here are the words and their motions:

Words	**Motions**
Jack-in-the-box.	Move the left arm in a circle counterclockwise around the front of the body.
Jack-in-the-box.	Move the left arm in a circle counterclockwise around the front of the body.
Open the lid.	Move the left arm in a circle counterclockwise around the front of the body. Bend down as it crosses over.

Words	Motions
And up he (she) pops.	Jump up.
Jack-in-the-box.	Move the right arm in a circle clockwise around the front of the body.
Jack-in-the-box.	Move the right arm in a circle clockwise around the front of the body.
Open the lid.	Move the right arm in a circle clockwise around the front of the body. Bend down as it crosses over.
And up he (she) pops.	Jump up.

How to Play: Stand next to your child. As you say the words, explain the corresponding actions. Show him how to take his left hand and cross it over in front of his body straight to the right side. As you say, "Jack-in-the-box," show him how to make it circle counterclockwise around to the left side and go back again in front of his body on the right side. Repeat. Do the same motion as you say, "Open the lid," but this time tell him to bend down as his arm comes back to the right side. Then when you say, "And up he (she) pops," tell him to jump up. Repeat explaining the rhyme using the right arm and the words that go with the right arm. Then do the singing and the motions of the song again together. Help him as much as is necessary to do the proper movements.

Jack-in-the-Box.

Meeting the Midline

7. Midline Matching

Objective: To teach your child how to develop midline awareness by matching picture halves.

About the Game: You can use pictures that you find in magazines or make your own drawings. Look for or draw something

I matched it!

that lends itself to being cut in half vertically. Some examples are faces, a lamp, a bowl, a person, and a tree. There are many more.

How to Play: Have some carefully selected pictures cut in two. Then ask your child to put the two parts together.

8. Roll a Ball

Objective: To teach your child midline awareness by rolling a ball straight and following it as it rolls.

About the Game: This game relates back to an old-time activity. Children have always enjoyed rolling a ball back and forth to each other. To accurately roll it, your child must look at the midline of the person opposite him and then roll it slowly. Your child will also get the built-in practice of following it with his eyes.

How to Play: Sit about four feet away from your child with your feet apart. Ask him to open his feet too. You can judge the proper distance by what feels comfortable for both of you. Then roll the ball back and forth as straight as possible between you. Watch the ball as it rolls to you and ask your child to watch it when it rolls to him. Whoever rolls should look straight ahead at the other person before starting.

9. Leg and Arm Balance

Objective: To teach your child midline awareness by balancing with opposite parts of the body.

About the Game: Your child must be midline centered to be able to lift up opposite parts of the body at the same time.

How to Play: Get down on the floor on all fours with your child and do the exercise opposite him. First lift your left leg and your right arm and ask him to do the same. After maintaining your balance in that position, switch sides and lift your right leg and your left arm. Have him do that too. Both of you should try to maintain your balance for five to ten seconds. You can do this several times if you wish. With practice you will both be able to hold the positions longer.

If it is too difficult to maintain balance in the beginning, you can modify the game to start. Instead of lifting the opposite arms and legs, lift the same arms and legs. When you and he become comfortable with that, begin working with the opposite sides. Another idea to help beginning balance is to hold hands as you each lift your arms in the air. As your balance improves, you can release your hands.

10. Row, Row, Row Your Boat

Objective: To teach your child midline awareness by moving back and forth in a straight-line motion.

About the Game: This is fun because you do it together with your child and sing at the same time. The more you let your child pull you, the more he will develop his sense of midline awareness. The straighter you both stay as you move back and forth, the more effective the exercise will be.

How to Play: Sit opposite each other on the floor. Open your legs wide and have your child place his legs inside yours. Join hands and move back and forth to the words of the song "Row, Row, Row Your Boat." You can go faster each time you sing, but do not go so fast that you will get out of alignment or that you might jerk each other's neck muscles in a rough way.

11. Jumping Jacks

Objective: To teach your child midline awareness by doing jumping jacks.

About the Game: This exercise has a particular form to it that is especially helpful in developing midline awareness. The hands come together over the head directly at the midline, and the feet also come together at the midline.

How to Play: Stand opposite your child in a position ready to do jumping jacks. Show your child the exact form for doing this exercise. Then work on his perfecting one. It goes like this: Feet apart, hands up above your head; feet together, hands down at your sides. Once he gets one right, increase the exercise to five. Then continue increasing the number of jumping jacks each time you play. You and your child will know how many are enough each time.

12. Patty-Cake

Objective: To teach your child midline development by meeting at the midline and by crossing it.

About the Game: This is one version of an age-old children's song passed down from generation to generation that provides midline awareness through using the hands and arms. The more practice your child has with this song, the better he will be able to do the movements. The easiest motion for the beginning of the rhyme is clapping each other's hands together, but when he is ready, you can show him how to cross clap with you. In that way he will have the opportunity to cross the midline of his body with his hands. Here are the words and their corresponding motions.

Words	**Motions**
Patty-cake, patty-cake, baker's man.	Clap together or cross clap several times.
Bake me a cake as fast as you can.	Continue to clap together or cross clap.
Roll it.	Move your arms around and around each other.
And stir it.	Place your hands together in front of you and move them around in a clockwise direction.
And mark it with a (child's initial).	Use your forefinger to mark the first initial of your child's name on your palm. Have your child mark the initial on his palm.
And toss it in the oven for (child's name) and me.	Make a tossing motion with your hands.

How to Play: Sit opposite your child and do the singing and motions of the song together. Help him as much as is necessary to do the proper movements. For clapping together you each do one clap on your own and then extend your opposite hands

Patty-Cake.

to meet straight ahead. For cross clapping you each do one clap on your own and then extend one hand to meet diagonally, do one clap on your own and then repeat with the other hand. The rest of the motions are more directly acting out the actions of the rhyme.

PART THREE

Social Development

Social development refers to relationship development. Between birth and age five your child develops the all-important relationship with himself. However strong and comfortable that becomes is what will determine how well he will be able to enter into strong and comfortable relationships with others.

The family is the training ground for all future relationships. All of the extended family relationships help your child to become who he will become. Grandparents, siblings, aunts, uncles, and cousins all play significant roles in your child's development. These roles need not be limited to family members, but it is important that someone is playing as many of each of these roles as possible. These roles represent people of all ages and of both genders. They also represent a range of personalities with varying degrees of passiveness and dominance. Exposure to all of these different types of people as part of a nurturing, loving, and caring family is what will help your child grow into a strong and healthy person. Of all these relationships, the parent-child is the first and most important.

As a parent you begin building your relationship with your child at birth. You start in a position of total control and move slowly throughout your child's life to a position of little or no control at around eighteen years of age. The whole process beginning on the first day is one of relinquishing control to your child. Day by day you are helping him to learn more and more about taking care of himself. While parents often get caught up in trying to control their child, this thinking about gradually transferring the control should make the process easier.

During this time you will see your child turning his attention from toys to games. He has more of an awareness of others and expresses enjoyment in interacting with others. At home, the focus of this play will be with family members and close friends. You will find the multitude of games in this book both handy and helpful. While each game is designed to foster a particular area of development, they are also designed for optimal adult-child interaction. At preschool or in the homes of others, the majority of your child's play will be with other children. Cooperative play is now in progress.

With so many skills developed and more developing, your child may begin showing interest in art, music, dance, and drama. If you notice that your child has a talent in one or more of these areas, you should do whatever is in your means to encourage it. Many adults who are accomplished in the arts trace their introduction to their area of expertise to these early years.

The categories for this topic are social skills, art, music, and drama. Activities in each of these four areas facilitate communication, interactions with others, reaching out to others, and relationship building. There are tremendous opportunities for growth in these areas, and this is the best time to begin.

7

Games for Social Skills

Simply put, social skills are the tools for getting along with others. While it may seem that the best teaching is done in the presence of other children, the best teaching is done through building self-esteem. If your child feels good about himself, he is likely to treat others nicely. If he does not feel good about himself, he is likely to treat others in a negative way. There are many ways that you can continually help your child in this area.

There are two important attitudes to have about your child all the time—respect and appreciation. A major way to show respect to your child is by using the word "please." A major way to show appreciation is by using the words "thank you." The way to teach your child to say "please" and "thank you" is by saying "please" and "thank you" to your child.

While your child will find himself in a world of comparison and competition with others, you can be the one to continually emphasize his uniqueness. You can be the one to call it to his attention as much as possible. This should not be too hard because no two people are alike. Each child is born into the world with a destiny to contribute something new and wonderful to the world. How exciting it is to be the one to guide and support your child toward this understanding of himself.

Your child may also find himself in a world of criticism and punishment. Try not to add to that picture. As a parent you have the opportunity to be the teacher of social behavior. If something goes wrong, the best plan is to recognize the situation, separate it out from your child, and teach him how not to make the same mistake again. In addition, try to learn yourself how you might be able to avoid this same situation from happening again in the future. We live and learn everyday. Make sure that you and your child both clearly understand that very special part of your important relationship.

The following games related to social skills building have been developed from these three important aspects of the self-esteem-building process—respect and appreciation, uniqueness, and mistakes of behavior.

Respect and Appreciation

1. The Please Game

Objective: To teach your child to give and receive respect by using the word "please."

About the Game: You can play this game at home or in any setting where you and your child have time to spend together.

How to Play: Take turns thinking up sentences to say to each other using the word "please" in each sentence. Here are some examples:

Please pass the book.

- Please pass the book.
- Please tie my shoe.
- Please hold my hand.
- Please read me a story.

Take turns and have fun thinking up different actions you would like each other to do.

2. The Thank You Game

Objective: To teach your child to give and receive appreciation by using the words "thank you."

About the Game: You can play this game at home or in any setting where you and your child have time to spend together.

How to Play: This is the time to surprise each other with thoughtful actions. Take turns thinking up nice things that you can do for one another. After something is done for you, be sure to say the words "thank you." Here are some ideas:

- Bring your child his favorite book.
- Your child may give you a big hug.
- Bring your child a piece of paper and a set of crayons for coloring.
- Your child may bring you a magazine that you like to read.

3. Working Together

Objective: To teach your child to work well with another person.

About the Game: Use any building set for this activity. Readily available ones are building blocks, Bristle Blocks, sponge letters or numbers, Lego, Tinkertoys, Lincoln Logs, a bottle cap collection, or others that you may have.

How to Play: Take turns building a structure. Each one of you add a piece and let the other add one after that. It should be interesting and fun what you two can create together.

4. Play a Game

Objective: To teach your child to play a simple game.

About the Game: You cannot play a game by yourself. You need someone to play with you. If you decide to select the game, be sure to start by saying to your child something like this, "Please play _____ with me." If your child selects the game, be sure to explain that he cannot play alone and to say to you something like "Please play _____ with me." At the end of the game, see who remembers to say first something like, "Thank you for playing with me."

How to Play: There are many types of possible games from which to choose. Lotto is probably the simplest. There is also dominoes, many versions of concentration, various board games like Candy Land and Chutes and Ladders, and Bingo. There are also simple playing card games like War, Go Fish, and Old Maid. There is also the well-known homemade paper game called Squares in which you each take turns connecting dots on a grid as you try to make actual squares. Begin the play of your chosen game. Offer your child as much help as is necessary for him to play.

Because games involve competition, this is a good time to talk about winning and losing. You can explain about skill and how it takes practice to learn how to play a game and to get better at it. You can also teach about luck and the roll it plays in most games. Here are some fun sentences to teach and repeat as you play:

- It doesn't matter if you win or lose, it's how you play the game.
- If at first you don't succeed, try, try again.

Uniqueness

5. I Like . . .

Objective: To teach your child about his uniqueness.

About the Game: As you point out to each other what you like about the other person, you will each gain new insight into some of your own uniqueness.

How to Play: Sit opposite each other and tell each other what you like about each other. Here are some examples.
    To your child you can say:

- I like the way you hold my hand.
- I like your smile.
- I like the twinkle in your eye.

Your child might say to you:

- I like your long hair.
- I like the way you hug me.
- I like your big, black purse.

6. My Favorite

Objective: To teach your child awareness of his own likes and dislikes.

About the Game: You can play this game in different rooms in your house.

How to Play: Go around to different room areas together. Maybe you can look at a whole wall or at a section of it. Take turns picking out what you like the best. Your child might say, "I like the painting." You might say, "I like the dish." You can play this at a table. Your child might say, "I like the vase." You might say, "I like the candlesticks." You can even play this by

I like the painting.

looking out the window. Your child might say, "I like the big tree." You might say, "I like the flowers."

7. Just Like Me

Objective: To teach your child about his own self-image.

About the Game: Look through a magazine together. Preferably find one that has in it pictures of both children and adults.

How to Play: As you look through each page, identify each person you see as:

- Just like me.
- Not like me.
- Almost like me.

Feel free to have lots of conversation about the people. You can have fun saying what it is about the people that makes them seem either like or not like you.

8. Foods, Toys, and Animals

Objective: To teach your child about his likes and dislikes.

About the Game: You may need several different kinds of magazines to cut out enough pictures of items in these three categories. Catalogues from stores are also good for this activity.

How to Play: Cut out pictures of foods, toys, and animals and divide them into categories. Then have fun taking turns picking pictures from one of the categories one at a time. As you each pick up a picture from one category, say, "I like it" or "I don't like it." When you have finished going through all the pictures in one category, go on to the next.

Mistakes of Behavior

9. Cooking Together

Objective: To teach your child some cooking skills and learn about mistakes at the same time.

Not like me.

About the Game: Cooking together is a wonderful parent-child activity. It will give you the opportunity to be aware of mistakes and to use them as a teaching opportunity.

How to Play: Set up some simple cooking activities. Beginning with the word "please" each time, give your child directions for the cooking activity. Here are some samples:

Making English Muffin or Bagel Pizzas

- Please pour on a tablespoon of pizza sauce.
- Please sprinkle on the grated cheese.
- Please place the pizzas on the toaster oven tray.

Making a Fruit Salad

- Please add the cantaloupe pieces.
- Please add the honeydew melon pieces.
- Please add the strawberries.
- Please add the blueberries.
- Please add the grapes.
- Please mix the salad.

Making Peanut Butter Shape Sandwiches

- Please spread the peanut butter on the bread.
- Please use cookie cutters to cut shapes in the bread.

Cooking with children often provides opportunities for the children not to follow some directions or for them to misbehave in the process. Practice interpreting all the misbehavior as mistakes of behavior and take each instance as an opportunity to teach your child how not to make the same mistake again.

10. Putting Toys Away

Objective: To teach your child to put his toys away.

About the Game: As part of living in a family, each member has specific responsibilities.

How to Play: Explain to your child how helpful it is when he puts away his own toys at the end of the day. A suggested way to do cleanup is with large plastic crates. Your child can sort the toys by color, or use some other system for placing toys in the crates. If he is unable or unwilling to follow through with this job, use some strategies that he might try the next time. Here are some ideas:

- Use toys from only one crate at a time so that cleanup will be easier.
- Put on a timer for cleanup time and see if he can beat the timer.
- Suggest taking turns with a brother or sister or friend picking up one item at a time.
- Play special music that he likes while he is putting his toys away.

You may have some of your own techniques that you can use to help your child.

11. Doll Play

Objective: To teach your child about the importance of behaving well.

About the Game: Having your child be like a parent to a doll will enhance his understanding of the parent-child role and the importance of trying to follow his parent's directions.

How to Play: Ask your child to go get a favorite doll. Then tell him to play with the doll for five minutes and to teach his doll about good behavior. Then ask him what he and his doll did and what lessons of behavior he taught his doll.

I could have asked for the ball.

12. Reflecting Together

Objective: To teach your child how to learn from mistakes of behavior in order to be able to do better in the future.

About the Game: It is pleasant to spend some time together at the end of the day reflecting on the day.

How to Play: Sit together on a couch or in some other comfortable place that is conducive to a quiet conversation and bonding. Have your child bring up incidents that happened during the day that did not go so well. You might have to be the one to bring up some or all of the incidents. Ask him to explain what happened. Then try to help him to figure out how he could have acted differently. Make this a positive time together, one full of nurturing and love. The sole purpose is teaching.

8

Games for Art

Social development is all about communication. While language is the best-known form of communication, there are others. Art is one of them. As with language development, art has a sequence in which it develops. In addition, just like language, art is carried out in many ways. Finally, as with language, art is a way of expressing both thoughts and feelings.

It is a good idea to have an art area. Because art can be a relatively messy activity, it is helpful to be all set up for the mess. You might want to have an easel and/or a table in an area with newspapers covering the floor underneath it. Moreover, it is important to this area concept that your child feel relaxed and independent, that he have a choice and be able to participate in projects that are open-ended and creative. Here are some suggested supplies:

- Variety of paper—construction paper, newsprint, copy paper, fax rolls, wallpaper scraps, and wrapping paper pieces.
- Variety of items—paper plates, foam trays, and index cards of different sizes.
- Glue and/or paste and Popsicle sticks or tongue depressors.
- Play dough or clay with rolling pins, cookie cutters, and craft sticks.
- Cardboard boxes, toilet paper and paper towel tubes, large material scraps, recyclable items, leaves, rice, and noodles.
- Safety scissors.
- Any safe and imaginable item that can be glued, colored, or cut.

Art is a powerful process with far-reaching capacities. It engages many senses and is a process that helps to integrate both hemispheres of the brain. It is also a series of motor movements that directly impact brain development. In addition, it includes thinking and problem-solving skills. Moreover, art evokes emotions that spark feelings of pleasantness and enjoyment.

When we think of art for children, we usually focus on the creative aspect of it, communicating a message through the skill of design. While this is the major part of the art process, there are other parts. There is the history of art, cultures of art, and the ability to be able to evaluate and appreciate art. These are all important to the entire subject area.

"Art" is defined in the *American Heritage Dictionary of the English Language* (p. 103) as "The conscious production or arrangement of sounds, colors, forms, movements, or other elements in a manner that affects the sense of beauty, specifically the production of the beautiful in a graphic or plastic medium."

The following games are taken from three basic areas of art—graphics with crayons, markers, paint, and chalk; sculpting with play dough, clay, and putty; and three-dimensional designs.

Graphics

1. Crayon Play

Objective: To teach your child to draw beautiful designs and pictures.

About the Game: With simple crayons and white or drawing paper, you and your child can have fun creating.

How to Play: Fold the paper in quarters. In each quarter draw a different symbol. Suggested examples are: dot, line, squiggle, circle, square, question mark, letters of the alphabet, numbers, and more. Have fun creating a design from each symbol. Be sure to work on your own drawing as well.

2. Pass the Art

Objective: To teach your child to draw creative designs with markers.

About the Game: By sharing the art designs, you and your child will experience increased stimulation for the creative process.

How to Play: Pass out three folded eight-and-a-half by eleven inch sheets of paper each to yourself and your child. Set a kitchen timer for two minutes. Draw with markers on your own

Creating with crayons.

paper during that time. When the timer rings, take your next paper and begin drawing with markers again. Do this same process a third time. Then exchange papers. Set up the timer again and continue adding artistic designs to your new set of papers, working on each one for two minutes just as before. Continue to pass the papers and work on the art until you both feel the artistic productions are finished.

3. Paint

Objective: To teach your child how to be artistic with paint.

About the Game: You can participate in this activity with whatever paint setup you have—easel, paints on a table, or even a small watercolor pallet.

How to Play: Set up the paint area for your child with water for cleaning the brush after using each color. Turn on the classical music of your choice and paint as the music moves you. Have fun painting your own picture as well.

4. Chalk

Objective: To teach your child how to do creative art with chalk.

About the Game: This simple medium is often overlooked.

How to Play: Take black construction paper and chalk, colored or white. Then create. It is just that simple. Enjoy your own artwork as well.

Sculpting

5. Sculpting in the Kitchen

Objective: To teach your child how to create with play dough, clay, or putty.

About the Game: Free-form creating with play dough, clay, or putty is fine. Use whichever material you have on hand. All are good for fine-motor development. If you think your child might enjoy a more structured experience, take out some small plastic bowls, cups, or dishes from your pantry for copying. Child-size or doll-size objects are recommended.

How to Play: Set up a paper towel place mat for each of you. Then take your own sculpting material and begin to create. If your child is interested, set one of the kitchen items down in front of your child and take one for yourself. Have fun trying to sculpt an object similar to the one you selected. Feel free to try more than one at a sitting.

6. Coil Pottery

Objective: To teach your child to make pottery designs by making coils and then molding them.

About the Game: Rolling play dough, clay, or putty develops finger muscles.

How to Play: Set up paper towel place mats for you and your child. Select the material of your choice and roll it with your fingers into long, thin strips. Then take a strip and wrap it around to make a coil. Then mold the coil into a bowl. Help your child as much or as little as is necessary. Then use another coil to make a cup. Use these coils to make as many bowl and cup designs as you would like. Participate in this activity as much as you would like. Feel free to extend the concept to making a table setting for your child's favorite group of dolls or stuffed animals.

7. Flat Shapes

Objective: To teach your child how to make sculpted designs using cookie cutters.

About the Game: Patting or using a rolling pin develops hand muscles.

I can roll snakes.

How to Play: Use paper towel place mats. Select your sculpting medium and then either pat the material flat or use a rolling pin. Take cookie cutters and press out different shapes. Take turns with your child both selecting and cutting out the shapes.

8. Molding

Objective: To teach your child how to use molds for this kind of medium.

I can cut designs.

About the Game: You will need some disposable items for this activity. For these materials, the mold will stay as part of the finished work. The entire project is good for hand and finger development.

How to Play: Collect some items that will make some interesting beginning shapes. Here are some ideas: small balls, small blocks, small plastic bottles, small plastic containers, small books, plastic cutlery, and paper cups. You will probably think of others. Cover the item in the sculpting material. Continue to create from there. You might want to decorate the finished product with large buttons, ribbons, or other items of your choice that are safe and not too small to swallow. Be sure to make your own creation while your child makes his.

Three-Dimensional Designs

9. Masks

Objective: To teach your child how to make a mask out of simple materials.

About the Game: Pretend play is the focus of this activity. Recommended materials are either nine-inch paper plates or paper bags (not plastic).

How to Play: Put the paper plate or the bag up to your child's face. Mark in pencil where you will need to cut out the eyes, nose, and mouth areas. Be careful not to poke your child as you select your places. Go through the same process making a mask for yourself. Then you and your child begin the creative process together. Use crayons, markers, construction paper cutouts, and yarn to design your own original masks. You can make them as wild or as simple as you like.

The paper bag mask will be ready to slip over your child's head when the decorating is completed. The paper plate can be finished by stapling the ends of a cut rubber band to each side of the plate or by attaching a tongue depressor at the bottom with strong masking or packing tape. Help your child as much as is necessary. When you are finished, let the fun begin. Play act with each other as you wear your new creations.

10. Butterflies

Objective: To teach your child how to make a butterfly from a coffee filter.

About the Game: In addition to a coffee filter, you will need a clothespin, Q-Tips, food coloring, and several small paper cups for making food-coloring solutions. It would also be a good idea to put out some paper towels or newspapers on your work surface to protect it from possible food-coloring stains.

How to Play: In small paper cups, make a variety of food-coloring solutions. Mix a few drops of food coloring with water to make several colors available. Then show your child how to dip a Q-Tip in the food-coloring solution of his choice and how to dab it on the coffee filter to make a design. Explain to him that he can use as many colors as he would like and to let them run together to enhance his design.

As soon as it is dry, scrunch it up into the shape of a butterfly and then clip it in the middle with a clothespin to make it into a butterfly. Make one for yourself while your child is working on his.

11. Appreciating Art

Objective: To teach your child to observe art and to appreciate it.

About the Game: Your knowledge and appreciation of art will determine the depth of this activity.

How to Play: Take your child on an art tour in your house. Go over to each painting or picture on your walls. Talk about what you see. If you know about the artist, the history connected with the picture, the culture, or anything about the painting or picture, explain it to your child. Encourage your child to tell you what he notices and all about his likes and dislikes. Share

Place mats.

thoughts and ideas and, most of all, have fun on your tour. Try not to make it too long or too short. Stay with this activity as long as you perceive it is holding your child's interest.

12. Place Mats

Objective: To teach your child how to make simple place mats.

About the Game: You can make a simple woven style by using two sheets of construction paper in different colors or make a plain table-setting mock-up on one sheet of paper.

How to Play: For the woven mat, use a pencil and draw one-inch lines on each sheet of construction paper. On one sheet draw them the long way, and on the other sheet draw them the short way. Cut the short strips through and cut the long ones leaving a one-inch border. Fold the sheet in half with the long strips drawn to make it easier to cut. Then weave the short strips into the paper with the long cuts on it. Make a mat for yourself and help your child with his as much as is necessary. Make as many mats like this as you wish and, of course, have fun using them.

For the plain mat, make a mock place mat. On this one use double-sided tape to tape down a plastic or paper plate and plastic utensils and a napkin. Making a mock-up like this is a nice way to teach table-setting skills.

9

Games for Music

Music is an important area of communication and self-expression. It gives a message of feelings. There are many different kinds of music. The finest quality is classical music. This fine music provides an excellent listening introduction to music for any child. There are variations of classical music in every culture. Examples are Tibetan flute music or Brazilian folk music. Singing and dancing to music also provides rich experiences for children. Another wonderful aspect of music comes from hearing, playing, and learning about musical instruments. Music is an entire area of enrichment for a child, and it can also be used to enhance many learning endeavors.

Classical music has been given new publicity as a technique for making children smarter. There is some truth to this concept, but it needs to be explained. One aspect is that it can make your child smarter in the sense that he can learn to recognize it. Just the act of recognizing something is an act that helps your child to continue to learn. The more he knows, the more he will increase his capacity to know more. Learning is recorded in the brain by synaptic links.

Don Campbell, author of *The Mozart Effect,* is among those credited with explaining the many different benefits of classical music. He found evidence that listening to Mozart's music impacts speech development, movement, and logical thinking skills. It is important to note that the effects of classical music last longer in preschool children than in college students.

People learn music by repetition and familiarity. Therefore, by repeatedly listening to a piece, your child will come to recognize it. It is recommended to play one piece over and over with your child, name the piece and composer for your child, and to continue the process until you have a sense that your child recognizes the piece and has learned it. Then it will be time to introduce another piece in the same way.

Other music plays a role for children as well. There are many simple tunes that children will pick up easily and enjoy. If the sounds communicate good feelings to your child, he will have a positive experience. Much loud rock or rap music gives a disturbing message and does not make a positive contribution to the lives of young children. Very loud music can actually cause hearing loss by damaging your child's middle ear. Presenting a variety of music is beneficial. It gives you the opportunity to point out its many facets. There are high parts and low ones, fast parts and slow tempos, dramatic parts and soothing strains, and many more aspects that are meaningful to discover. Rhythm is a very important aspect of this experience.

Singing music is a worthwhile activity for children. Singing to them in the early years lays the groundwork for their being able to sing. Even if you think you cannot sing well, it is beneficial to sing to your child. More important than the exact tune or words is the loving feeling you express. Your singing is also a form of language stimulation. Besides enjoying the activity, he will learn from the words at the same time.

Dancing brings with it another dimension of music. First, there is the fun of moving to music. Then there is the exercise. In addition, there is the creativity development connected with moving to music. When two children dance together, mirroring movements of each other, swinging their arms together, and holding hands, they also have a nice way to enjoy each other as well as the music.

Musical instruments play a role as well. Children can learn to recognize different instruments and their sounds. They can also learn to play them. In addition they can make their own instruments.

"Music" is defined in the *American Heritage Dictionary of the English Language* (p. 1190) as "The art of arranging sounds in time so as to produce a continuous, unified, and evocative composition, as through melody, harmony, rhythm, and timbre."

The following games are taken from four basic areas of music—listening to music, singing, dancing, and musical instruments.

Listening to Music

1. Classical Music of Your Choice

Objective: To teach your child to recognize one piece of classical music from one composer.

About the Game: The particular piece you select is not as important as the fact that you like it. The important point is that you will enjoy listening to it and be able to communicate some of your knowledge and enthusiasm for it to your child. Many pieces by Beethoven, Mozart, Brahms, and Chopin often appeal to young children. High-quality music from your particular culture can be substituted as well. It will have the added benefit of adding to your child's cultural identity.

How to Play: Select the music of your choice. Then play it as often as you can—in the car, during a meal, or as background during quiet play. Point out loud and soft parts and parts with fast and slow tempos. If it comes naturally, hum along with specific passages as you get to know them.

2. Children's Music of Your Choice

Objective: To teach your child to recognize and enjoy simple music geared to young children.

About the Game: The music you select should be chosen for its pleasant tones and for the simple concepts it teaches. There are many CDs available with all kinds of children's songs. If you have a singer you know and like, select that music. Otherwise select pieces that teach simple concepts or tell simple stories. This easy-to-follow music will help your child enjoy music and continue to learn many different kinds of information.

How to Play: Follow the suggestions for classical music. Select the music of your choice. Then play it as often as you can—in the car, during a meal, or as background during quiet play. Point out interesting parts and, if you wish, hum or sing along with specific passages as you get to know them.

Listening to music.

3. Drawing to Music

Objective: To teach your child to appreciate music by drawing pictures to it and by using colors that describe it.

About the Game: One tape is especially designed for this activity. It is called *The Mozart Effect, Music for Children, Relax, Daydream, and Draw*, Volume 2, compiled by Don Campbell. (See the bibliography for more information.) However, any classical or cultural music will work well. The more you play this game, the more different musical pieces you can introduce.

How to Play: Give your child drawing paper and crayons or markers. Turn on the music of your choice. Tell your child to draw whatever the music brings to mind. Suggest that he choose particular colors that seem to go with the music. Be sure to take a sheet of paper for yourself as well and enjoy the same activity. You can talk to each other as you draw or talk after you finish drawing and explain to each other all about your pictures.

Singing

4. Sing-along

Objective: To teach your child to sing along with music that has words.

About the Game: There are many sing-along programs that you can buy. If you have singing music without a words book, consider making your own.

How to Play: Share the words book or your homemade version with your child. As you sing together, point to each of the words as you sing them. This will enhance your child's reading skills and also add to the correctness of how he pronounces the words.

5. Singing to Your Child

Objective: To teach your child how to sing and enjoy singing.

About the Game: Just as talking to your child teaches your child to talk, and reading to your child teaches reading, singing to your child teaches your child how to sing. As you model these activities, do them in a nurturing way. That nurturing is an important part of the process.

How to Play: Sing songs that you know to your child. They do not have to be any particular ones. The best will be those that you remember from your childhood. Feel free to add others that you like that you have learned. Songs with finger plays and hand motions are always popular. Nursery rhymes, poems, and chants also fit into this category. Rhythm is part of the whole process.

You can also let your child take the lead in this activity. He may know some common songs like "The Wheels on the Bus," "Twinkle, Twinkle Little Star," "The Alphabet Song," "Ten Little Indians," and "If You're Happy and You Know It." There are many, many more. Join in with your child when he sings. In addition, suggest some songs that he knows and have some fun singing them together. Use hand motions to go with the songs or clap to the music to make them into as much of a lively activity as possible.

6. Make Up Songs

Objective: To teach your child to use music to learn important information.

About the Game: Putting words to tunes helps children to learn specific information.

How to Play: Make up words for tunes for your child to learn simple facts like his telephone number, his address, and other important information.

(914) 948-4271.

Dancing

7. Dancing

Objective: To teach your child to be creative with music.

About the Game: Children enjoy moving to music. When they make up their own steps, they feel great satisfaction. They also get valuable exercise from this activity.

How to Play: Select a CD with lively music. You can also turn on the radio. Take turns doing different dance routines. In addition, try some dances that you make up together.

I can dance.

8. Dancing to Directions

Objective: To teach your child specific dance steps and movements.

About the Game: Use CDs that give specific directions for dances and other movements. There are many available, such as those by Hap Palmer and Ella Jenkins. If you do not have these or other similar ones available, play other music and try making up your own directions as your child dances. In addition, you can encourage your child to make up directions for you.

How to Play: Play the CD with directions on it and enjoy following the directions together. If you are using regular music without directions, call some out. Here are some examples of things you might say:

- Sway with the music.
- Clap to the music.
- March to the music.

9. Dancing Songs

Objective: To teach your child specific movements and dances.

About the Game: There are many childhood games that have specific movements to learn. Examples are "The Hokey Pokey" and "Here We Go Round the Mulberry Bush." In addition, you may know some simple dances that you can teach to your child like square dancing or ethnic dances.

How to Play: Teach whatever specific movement games and dances you know. Participate in the activity as you teach.

Musical Instruments

10. Simple Musical Instruments

Objective: To teach your child how to play simple musical instruments.

About the Game: There are many simple instruments available for young children. You might already have a special one. Some suggestions are drums, maracas, tambourines, triangles, and bells.

How to Play: Using a CD or the radio, turn on some interesting rhythmic music. Use whatever instrument you have to keep time to the music. Take turns using it or use two different instruments and play music together.

11. Homemade Musical Instruments

Objective: To teach your child how to make and use homemade musical instruments.

About the Game: There is no limit to the kind of homemade instruments you and your child can make. Here are some suggestions:

- Shakers from plastic containers filled with rice, beans, or paper clips.
- Drums from plastic containers and chopsticks.
- Tambourines from paper plates with bells attached by yarn through hole-punched holes.

How to Play: Make some homemade instruments. Then turn on music from a CD or the radio and use the instruments to keep time to the music. Take turns using different instruments or use different ones at the same time.

12. Sophisticated Instruments

Objective: To teach your child about sophisticated instruments.

About the Game: Whatever resources you have will determine how this activity is carried out.

A flute.

How to Play: Take out any instrument you may have in your house. It could be a flute, clarinet, saxophone, trumpet, or violin, or it could be a piano or keyboard. If you do not have any, this would be a good time to get a book about instruments and use those pictures of instruments instead. Simply show the instrument, play it if you can, and explain it to the best of your ability. As you care for and value the instrument, you will be teaching your child how to care for it and value it as well.

10

Games for Drama

Drama plays a major role for children in the area of social skills development. Pretend play, the focus of drama in the early years, is life's theatrical stage for young children. It is the stage on which they have the opportunity to act out what they have already experienced as well as some scripts that they would like to experience.

There are many aspects to dramatics that are beneficial to young children in all areas of development. Through doing short skits, children have the opportunity to experience a part of life that they otherwise would not experience. For a glimpse of time they walk in someone else's shoes in a far-off place or in some other time. They also have the opportunity to feel successful. They can master a part and enjoy the satisfaction from it. Socially, they have the unique chance to work with others on a common goal, share materials, and help one another. Even physically there is the opportunity to take on some new challenges and pick up some new skills. Last but not least is language development. They have the opportunity to acquire vocabulary, both receptive and expressive, and to increase their attention span.

There are several different types of dramatic experiences that you can set up for your child. One stems from the opportunity to dress up. Another comes from ways to set up dramatic play areas. A third is through routine play, and a fourth comes from books, nursery rhymes, and songs.

"Drama" is defined in the *American Heritage Dictionary of the English Language* (p. 560) as "The quality or condition of being dramatic." "Dramatic" is defined in that dictionary as "Suggestive of acting or an emotional and often affected stage performance."

Dress Up

1. Going Out

Objective: To teach your child how to pretend about adult experiences.

About the Game: You will need old dresses, shirts, and pants for this activity and any accessories like necklaces, handbags, ties, and keys for this kind of play.

How to Play: Put out a selection of old clothes that your child can use for dress up. Then let your child take over from there. Explain to your child that you will first see him off to his favorite nightspot and that you will be there to welcome him back home. Ask questions that will help your child feel free to

A night out.

enjoy this pretend role. Here are some suggested questions for
on the way out:

- Where are you going?
- Who is going with you?
- Are you driving there or walking?

Here are some for the return:

- Did you go to a restaurant?
- Did you see a movie?
- How is your friend?

2. Dressing for the Occasion

Objective: To teach your child to pretend about normal child-hood experiences.

About the Game: Being able to dress appropriately is part of this creative activity. Children at this age like to change their clothes frequently. That will add to the fun.

How to Play: Explain to your child that you and he are going to pretend to go out to different places and that he will need to be wearing appropriate clothes for each place. Say a different place, one at a time. After each place say, "Dress for the occasion." Here are some suggested places:

- Picnic
- Swimming
- Skiing
- Shopping
- Out to dinner

Add other places as you think of them. After your child returns to you dressed for the occasion, discuss the outfit and the upcoming event. Encourage your child to dream his adventure with words like, "Close your eyes and tell me what you see, hear, touch, taste, and smell."

3. The Bedtime Plan

Objective: To teach your child a successful bedtime routine.

About the Game: Bedtime can be a difficult time for children in today's times. There are many reasons for this. One is the busy and rushed lifestyle of parents. They are tired at night and find it hard to stick to a calm and consistent ritual. Another is the hectic day many young children have. They can be in child-care settings away from their parents for long periods of time and in great need at night of spending high-quality time with their parents. A third is the ironic reason that many children are overtired at night because they do not get enough sleep. Few parents understand the vital role ten to eleven hours of sleep each night plays in their child's health and well-being. Here are some important facts about sleep:

- It regulates nerves and hormones.
- It affects the cardiovascular, gastrointestinal, and immune systems.
- It replenishes, stimulates, and organizes neurotransmitters. These are necessary for learning, problem solving, and creativity.
- It affects daily functioning—alertness, accident rates, communication skills, energy, learning, mood, performance, safety, and thinking.
- It enhances memory—particularly during REM sleep.

- It facilitates cell repair, which rejuvenates and energizes the brain.

How to Play: Tell your child to dress for bed. Encourage him to put on his favorite pajamas and get as comfortable as possible. Then create and act out together a mutually enjoyable bedtime routine. As part of your routine teach your child on his level how lucky he is to have a comfortable bed in a quiet place ready for him to rest, relax, and enjoy all the benefits of a complete night's sleep. If there are problems connected with this time, this play activity will serve as a wonderful opportunity to talk to him about the problems and to work them out while you are not in the real situation of nighttime and under the actual pressure to get your child to sleep.

Dramatic Play Areas

4. The Restaurant

Objective: To teach your child creative play related to food.

About the Game: Food and nutrition are a complicated issues for parents and children in today's times. While children are thrust into the world of junk food and experiencing food almost as play items, parents have the responsibility of feeding their children in a nutritious way. This game provides a wonderful opportunity for you and your child to come to terms with this situation and learn how to work together on it.

How to Play: Set up a play restaurant area. Use whatever resources you have and be as creative as you wish. Here are some starter ideas: a table and chairs with items on it like plastic cups, plates, and silverware, aprons, menus, a sign, tablecloth, place mats, napkins, a play telephone, and any other equipment you may have. Then enjoy your play together. You may want to talk about the food pyramid and the importance of eating fruits and vegetables. You may even want to create delicious and nutritious alternatives to the frequently served chicken fingers and hot dogs, which are so often served to children in restaurants. Have fun dining and serving each other in this interesting play setting.

5. The Health Club

Objective: To teach your child creative play related to exercise.

About the Game: Many children today do not get enough exercise. They spend sedentary lives in school and return home to watch many hours of television and videos. In addition, they are spending increasing amounts of time in front of a computer. Setting up a play health-club atmosphere will give you a chance to give your child important information about exercise and also to have fun experiencing it together.

How to Play: Set up a play health-club area. Use whatever resources you have and be as creative as you wish. Do not forget to dress the part. Here are some starter ideas: an exercise CD, a step for step aerobics, an easy chair to use as a pretend weight machine, some soup cans to use as pretend weights, and any other exercise props that you may have. Then enjoy your play together. One idea is to rotate from a pretend aerobics class to the weight machines and then to the weights themselves. Let the sky be the limit. Take a run together, do jumping jacks, participate in all kinds of stretches, sit-ups (crunch-style), and push-ups. Feel free to exchange ideas with each other about exercises that each of you know.

6. The Doctor's Office

Objective: To teach your child creative play related to general health.

About the Game: A well-known favorite for children is playing doctor. This is a good time to capitalize on that interest and teach some of the principles of maintaining good health at the same time.

How to Play: Set up a doctor's office area. Use whatever resources you have and be as creative as you wish. Do not forget to dress the part. Here are some starter ideas: a couch, bed, or cot, and items like a large white shirt, gauze, cotton, Band-Aids, a play telephone, a play doctor's bag, tongue depressors, dolls, and any other doctor props that you may have. Then enjoy your play together. One idea is to take turns being the doctor and the patient. When you are the doctor, explain to your child about the preventive medicine known as sleep, nutrition, and exercise. Talk about how good practices in these areas will help to keep your child from having colds, flu, and other sicknesses. This will be a great time to teach the famous saying, An apple a day keeps the doctor away. You both might even want to eat apples. Have fun doctoring each other up, but do not forget to have fun teaching each other important tricks of the trade for staying well.

The doctor is in.

Routine Play

7. Making a Tent

Objective: To teach your child to expand his pretend play capacity in the house.

About the Game: Store-bought toys are relatively new in the mass-produced way that we experience them today. As recent as the first part of the twentieth century, children made most of their toys and created most of their play and play areas. Pretend play engages the brain in every way. The free-form aspect of it is responsible for more learning than most planned activities. While thinking, planning, and carrying out plans are rich educational experiences, emotions enter into the picture as well.

How to Play: Find a corner somewhere and with a small blanket or sheet, turn it into a tent area for your child. Encourage him to bring toys of his choice and set up his own personal play area. No rules or instructions are needed here. With dolls, cars, building sets, and other toys of his choice, your child will know exactly what to do. Participate with your child as much as he and you desire. In addition, you can add stimulating sentences like some of these:

- What are you doing?
- Can I help you?
- Do you need something from the kitchen?
- Can you make room for some books, flowers, baskets, and so on?

8. Using a Blanket

Objective: To teach your child to expand his pretend play outside.

About the Game: While the house has many items in it that lend themselves to unlimited creative play, the outdoors presents other resources.

Inside the tent.

How to Play: Take a blanket outside and lay it out in a comfortable safe place. Suggest to your child that he use it in any
way he wishes. Maybe he would like to have a pretend picnic,
think of it as a swimming pool, or maybe set up a beach. Encourage him to collect twigs, branches, rocks, leaves, and other
materials to act out whatever play he decides to create. Participate as much as you and he would like. Add special questions
and comments that might enrich the play experience. Here are
some ideas:

- What delicious sandwiches do you make?
- Can I swim in your pool?
- Your beach pail is full of interesting rocks.

9. Puppets

Objective: To teach your child how to make and use puppets for pretend play.

About the Game: There are many simple materials available for making puppets.

How to Play: Look around for materials for making creative puppets. Here are some ideas: wooden spoons, Popsicle sticks, tongue depressors, gloves, mittens, paper and plastic plates, unsharpened pencils, and construction paper. Add to these tools and supplies like scissors, glue sticks, crayons, markers, yarn, fabric store eyes (not too small to swallow), and more. Once you have a collection of these kinds of materials, you and your child will be ready to create. Make as many interesting puppets as you would like. Once you are finished, take a look at what you have. Then, in the same open-ended manner, begin your own creative puppet play.

Books, Nursery Rhymes, and Songs

10. Act Out a Book

Objective: To teach your child how to experience the feelings of characters in a book.

About the Game: Choose a book that your child likes a lot and knows very well.

How to Play: Take turns acting out any character of your choice in a story. A good example is the well-known book *The*

Little Engine That Could. Take turns acting out the struggle of the train trying to get over the mountain. *Goldilocks and The Three Bears, Little Red Riding Hood,* and many, many others provide strong characters for dramatic play.

11. Nursery Rhyme Dramatics

Objective: To teach your child drama skills through well-known nursery rhymes.

About the Game: Many nursery rhymes lend themselves to great acting.

How to Play: Take turns choosing a rhyme and acting it out. Here are some popular examples: "Old King Cole," "Little Boy Blue," "The Itsy Bitsy Spider," "Little Miss Muffett," "Mary Had a Little Lamb," and "Jack Be Nimble." You may know many others.

12. Acting Songs

Objective: To teach your child some well-known songs that have creative acting parts.

About the Game: There are well-known circle songs that lend themselves to creative acting activities.

How to Play: Stand together and sing and play any of these kinds of songs: "Here We Go Round the Mulberry Bush," "The Hokey Pokey," and "Pop Goes the Weasel."

Circle game fun.

PART FOUR

Language Development

Of all the influences on children, language experiences are the ones that are most correlated with child academic success. Children exposed to a high degree of quality language will be the ones who are likely to achieve a high intellectual level. Whereas providing enriched language experiences used to be a problem only for those in low socioeconomic groups, it is now a universal problem. Parents at home are often too busy to have much language interaction with their child. In addition, many are away from their child for long periods of time. Caregivers who are with children for long periods of time often have too many children in their care to be able to provide them all with the necessary language stimulation so important to child development in the early years.

Language development takes place simultaneously in four areas—reading, writing, listening, and speaking. While our schools and culture emphasize the importance of reading, no one form of communication is more important than another. They all work together to enrich each other. When you understand more, you can both speak and read at a higher level. When you speak and read at a high level, you are able to understand more. These are all vocabulary, expressive-language, and comprehension-building skills.

There are many language activities that are pleasant for parents and their children and that have been carried out in different ways for centuries. Reading to and with children is one. Drawing and writing with children is another. Playing listening games that focus on sounds and words is a third. Reciting nursery rhymes, singing simple childhood songs, and reading out loud to children is a fourth.

The categories for this topic are reading, writing, listening, and speaking. These are the building blocks of literary skills and make up the process of communication. They are all interactive. When you read, you get a message that someone wrote. When you write, it is for someone to read. When you listen, it is because someone is speaking, and when you speak, it is to someone who is listening.

11

Games for Reading

One of the most time-honored and enjoyable child-care activities, passed on from generation to generation, is reading to a child. Reading is a natural part of our lifestyle and is something children should be aided in from the early years. Just as exposure to the spoken word leads to speech, exposure to the written word leads to reading.

Children learn to talk because people talk to them. In the same way they learn to read if people read to them. Books with large print are especially helpful in the beginning because you can easily point to the words as you read them. Try to point to the words you are reading in all books. This will help your child to connect the spoken word with its written form.

The repetition of seeing the same words in different books and in different places will lead to the recognition of those words. Because we have a culture filled with bright signs, those large words can also be used for reading enrichment.

Letter cards are a good way to learn letters, and word cards are good for learning words. Games with letters and their sounds combined with games with words and sentences will contribute to successful reading.

"Read" is defined in the *American Heritage Dictionary of the English Language* (p. 1504) as "to examine and grasp the meaning of (written or printed characters, words, or sentences).

The following games have been taken from these areas of reading—letters, words, sentences, and books and magazines.

Letters

1. Letter Cards

Objective: To teach your child the letters of the alphabet.

About the Game: Having a set of letter cards will provide you with many different ways to teach your child the letters.

How to Play: Make yourself a set of thirteen letter cards with the twenty-six letters placed back-to-back from A to Z. Use three-by-five-inch index cards as the base and place stick-on capital letters that you can get in an office supply store on the cards. Hole punch each card in one of the upper corners and tie twelve-inch yarn loops in each of those holes.

You can use the alphabet cards like toys. Hang them on doorknobs or other places or hide them for play. Trace your finger around each letter the way you would write it and show your child how to do the same. Place them on objects that start with the matching letter like a D on a doorknob, a B on a book, or a T on a table.

Alphabet cards.

2. Alphabet Song

Objective: To teach your child the letters as connected with the well-known alphabet song.

About the Game: Make an alphabet chart of the whole alphabet. Write out the letters in the format that goes with the tune of the song like this:

ABCD
EFG
HIJK

LMNOP
QRS
TUV
WXYZ
Now I know my ABC's
Next time won't you sing with me?

When you sing the song together, point to each letter as you sing it. You can also take turns with your child matching alphabet cards from the Letter Cards game to letters on the chart.

3. Alphabet Song II

Objective: To teach your child that the lowercase letters as connected with the well-known alphabet song.

About the Game: Make a lowercase alphabet chart of the whole alphabet. Write out the lowercase letters in the format that goes with the tune of the song like this:

abcd
efg
hijk
lmnop
qrs
tuv
wxyz
Now I know my ABC's
Next time won't you sing with me?

When you sing the song together, point to each letter as you sing it. You can also take turns with your child matching capital letter alphabet cards from the Letter Cards game to the lowercase letters on this chart.

Words

4. Word Cards

Objective: To teach your child words by sight.

About the Game: There are 100 words that are most frequently heard in the English language. These words make up 50 percent of all elementary school reading. The first ten make up 25 percent of all elementary school reading. They are all printed on the following chart. For this game, make your own word cards in duplicate on three-by-five-inch index cards. Start using a few card pairs and add more as your child masters them.

1. the	16. as	31. but	46. she
2. of	17. with	32. not	47. do
3. and	18. his	33. what	48. how
4. a	19. they	34. all	49. their
5. to	20. I	35. were	50. if
6. in	21. at	36. we	51. will
7. is	22. be	37. when	52. up
8. you	23. this	38. your	53. other
9. that	24. have	39. can	54. about
10. it	25. from	40. said	55. out
11. he	26. or	41. there	56. many
12. was	27. one	42. use	57. then
13. for	28. had	43. an	58. them
14. on	29. by	44. each	59. these
15. are	30. word	45. which	60. so

61. some	71. two	81. my	91. long
62. her	72. more	82. than	92. down
63. would	73. write	83. first	93. day
64. make	74. go	84. water	94. did
65. like	75. see	85. been	95. get
66. him	76. number	86. call	96. came
67. into	77. no	87. who	97. made
68. time	78. way	88. oil	98. may
69. has	79. could	89. now	99. part
70. look	80. people	90. find	100. over

How to Play: Concentration is an all-time favorite game for children. You can start with three pairs of words and later play with as many pairs as is appropriate for your child. Place the pairs mixed up facedown on the table. Have your child pick one card, turn it over, read it, and then pick another. If it matches, he keeps the pair and goes again. If not, he turns them both over, and you take your turn. You both try to remember where the cards are on the table. If your child has trouble reading a word, you can help him. After repetition of the game, your child will start to remember more and more words. The winner is the one with the most pairs.

Before or after playing Concentration, you might want to play a simple matching game. Lay out a few cards from one set of the cards and ask your child to match cards you give him one at a time.

For the rest of the games one set of cards is enough.

Place the word cards you have in a pile facedown. Take turns picking a card. If your child can read it, he can keep it. If not, he puts it at the bottom of the pile, and then it is your turn.

Place a few cards faceup on the table and read them to your child, pointing to each card as you read it. Then say you will read and make a mistake. Tell your child to say *stop* when he hears a mistake. Then tell your child to be the reader and to read some correctly and then to make a mistake.

Use the cards like flashcards. However, tell your child not to say the word until you hide the card behind your back. In this way he has to remember it and thus build his visual memory skills. In addition, there is less pressure to be right because the focus of the game is on remembering what he saw and not on reading correctly.

5. Hop, Jump, and Clap

Objective: To teach your child to read action words.

About the Game: This activity gives your child the opportunity to practice reading verbs. Being able to act out the words is helpful in the learning process. In addition, the element of surprise by picking each word adds to the fun.

How to Play: Start with three words—Hop, Jump, and Clap. Write each word on a three-by-five- or four-by-six-inch index card and place the cards facedown in a pile. Then take turns with your child picking a card and acting out the word. After he masters reading those three, add another. Each time you play, start with the ones already made. If he knows them well, add another verb. Suggested beginning words are: walk, run, jog, sleep, swim, talk, and sing. You may add others that you think your child will enjoy.

There are two other versions of this game that help to develop children's love for acting things out. These are with nouns, not verbs. For example, you could make a set of cards with different occupations on them. Suggested words are: fire fighter, police officer, doctor, lawyer, teacher, and secretary. You could also make a set of cards with names of animals on them. Your child can act out the animal including the animal sound. You can take your turn in these games as well.

6. Word Labels

Objective: To teach your child to read words that name items.

About the Game: Matching nouns to real items is usually of high interest to young children. It is an active process as well.

How to Play: Using three-by-five-inch index cards, make a set of word cards that go with items in your living room or bedroom. Here are suggestions: table, lamp, chair, sofa, rug, pillow, TV, and bed.

Have fun taking turns picking a card and placing it on the correct item. Then have fun taking turns returning the cards and putting them in a pile. Another version of the game is to put the cards out in the room in the wrong places and then enjoy taking turns replacing them correctly one at a time.

Sentences

7. This is a . . .

Objective: To teach your child to read sentences.

About the Game: This activity gives your child the chance to practice reading sentences while playing a labeling game. The

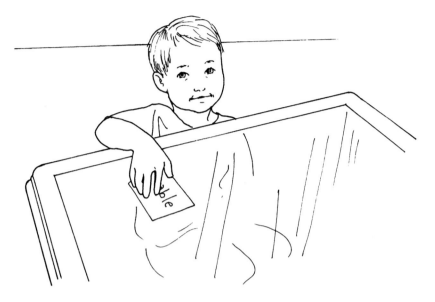

Here is a table.

element of surprise by picking each word card from a pile adds
to the fun.

How to Play: You can use the words from the Word Labels
game or make new ones. A suggestion is to start with these
three words—sofa, chair, and rug. Write each one on a three-
by-five-inch index card and place the cards in a pile. Take
turns with your child picking a card and placing it on the object named on the card. After he masters reading these three,
add another. Each time you play, start with the ones already
made. If he knows them well, add another word that goes with
something else in the room. Suggested beginning words are
table, lamp, wall, door, plant, window, and desk; but any item
of interest in the room is fine.

Next make the three sentence-starter cards—*This, is,* and *a.*
Then put them out on a table with a space and then an index

This is a table.

card with a period on it. Take turns picking a card to complete the sentence. Then take turns reading the sentence.

8. Message

Objective: To teach your child to read sentences.

About the Game: A blackboard with chalk, a marker message board with a marker, or plain paper and a pencil are all fine for this activity.

How to Play: On one of the boards or on a plain piece of paper, write an appropriate message, one sentence in length, for your child. Choose vocabulary that you think he will be able to read. You can start with an easy one and get progressively harder. One example is, "Good morning, (child's name)." Another is, "Have a good day, (child's name)." A third idea is to ask for an action like, "(Child's name), come here."

9. Short Directions

Objective: To teach your child to read sentences.

About the Game: Putting directions on cards creates a pleasant action activity and increases reading skills at the same time.

How to Play: Use four-by-six-inch cards for these directions. Make a set of simple three-word ones that you and your child can take turns carrying out. Try to think of short actions that will be fun to do. Here are some suggested samples:

- Open the door.
- Tie the shoe.
- Fold the napkin.
- Move the book.

Books and Magazines

10. Bookshelf Books

Objective: To teach your child to read by reading to him.

About the Game: At this stage of development, your child is probably competent in some beginning reading skills, but this is your time to pick up some higher level books. You can choose books from your home, a library, or a bookstore to introduce your child to thought-provoking situations that will help him grow in a social or educational way. Any book that your child responds to positively is appropriate because this is a time to share a quiet experience together. It will also serve to build receptive and expressive vocabulary for your child and the desire to improve his own reading level.

How to Play: Set up the books on your child's bookshelf for rotation. When you pick the one, two, or three for your reading session, take them from the left end and return them to the right end. This process will make all the books you choose to read seem new and interesting. Of course, if your child has a favorite, it is fine to read that one over and over again. Always try to introduce new books but do not force them on your child. That would defeat the whole purpose of a positive reading experience with your child.

If you find you are reading certain books over and over, here is an activity you can do while you read. You can leave out a word at the end of a sentence and see if your child can say it. If not, after a short pause, fill it in yourself. Be careful not to put your child on the spot. Maybe after more repetitions and at another time, he will be able to do it. Continue in this manner with other words in the book.

11. A Reading Book

Objective: To teach your child to read by reading books at his level.

About the Game: This game can be adapted to any level. If your child is not reading at all, use a book with interesting pictures and talk about them. If your child can read with just alphabet letters or numbers, use books with those in them. If you have some other books with large clear words that your child can identify, feel free to use those. It is the repetition of simple letters, numbers, words, phrases, or sentences that leads to reading success.

An alternative to this kind of reading experience is home-made books. You can take a small photo album and put pictures on one side and a descriptive word, phrase, or simple sentence on the other side. A personalized book about a trip or home activities will always be of high interest to your child. You can also cut apart a coloring book, paste pictures from it on construction paper pages inserted in a Duotang folder and make up a story with words that your child knows how to read. For these home-made books, you can use one word, two words, three words, or short sentences, whichever is most appropriate for your child.

How to Play: This is the time to share reading with your child on his reading level. Choose a book that he will enjoy and that is easy enough for him to feel successful and alternate reading. You take all the left-hand pages and he the right-hand pages or vice versa. Always point out the words that each of you are reading. Help your child as much or as little as is necessary.

12. Child's Magazine

Objective: To teach your child about enjoying magazines.

About the Game: For this age I recommend *Sesame Street* Magazine (P.O. Box 2896, Boulder, CO 80321), *My Weekly Reader for Kindergarten* (Xerox Education Publications, 1250 Fairwood Ave., Columbus, OH 43216), *Highlights for Children* (2300 West Fifth Avenue, P.O. Box 269, Columbus, OH 43216), and *Nick*

Reading a magazine.

Jr. (Nickelodeon Magazines, Inc., 1515 Broadway, New York, NY 10036).

How to Play: Subscriptions to these are nice for a child. Your child will enjoy receiving copies by mail. When they come, your child can review the magazine on his own and enjoy whatever pictures, words, or activities are on his level. Then when you have time to sit with your child, focus on whichever activities will be especially interesting and/or helpful to your child. Reading one of the stories to him can be especially beneficial.

12

Games for Writing

Writing skills develop through practice combined with the proper amount of fine-motor exercises. Because eye-hand coordination is an important part of writing success, many of the suggested games include copying tasks.

Learning to draw and learning to write are similar processes. They both start off with scribbles. Then in time they develop into full-fledged drawing and writing skills. The preparation for both skills is also similar—practice with writing on paper using crayons, markers, pencils, and pens. While they are both artistic endeavors requiring the ability to accurately represent what you have in mind, drawing branches out to creative representations, and writing narrows down to being representational of specific symbols.

Some of these games are found in different forms in workbooks found in school supply or discount stores. However, often they are designed on a level that is too difficult for a preschool-age child. Here you will enjoy the opportunity to design your own games in appropriate formats that you can tailor to your child's level. What you have will be personalized alternatives laid out in your own individual way.

"Write" is defined in the *American Heritage Dictionary of the English Language* (p. 2061) as "to form (letters, words, or symbols) on a surface such as paper with an instrument such as a pen."

"Draw" is defined in the same dictionary (p. 561) as "To inscribe (a line or lines) with a pencil or other marking implement."

The games that follow have been designed around learning progress in both drawing and writing skills.

Drawing

1. Copy and Color in Shapes

Objective: To teach your child to copy a simple shape and to color in the lines.

About the Game: Both copying and coloring in the lines are important skills connected with the drawing process. As these simple shapes are mastered, you can do the activity with more difficult shapes, giving your child a chance to learn more about shapes as well.

How to Play: Fold an eight-and-a-half-by-eleven-inch sheet of paper in four parts. Draw two shapes in the two upper sections. Ask your child to color them and then copy and color them in the two lower sections. Emphasize coloring in the whole shape.

If your child is ready, do the activity again with him drawing the shapes in the top two sections and you coloring them and then copying and coloring them in the lower sections.

Copying and coloring.

2. Picture Copying

Objective: To teach your child to copy a simple drawing.

About the Game: You can begin this game on a simple level and draw more advanced pictures with more detail as your child grows. A simple house with a tree and flowers is a good start. A whole landscape can be developed at a future time if your artist skills and your child's skills are up to it. Use your child's artistic level as a guide for how simple or complete your picture should be.

How to Play: Fold an eight-and-a-half-by-eleven-inch sheet of paper in half. Draw a picture on the top half and ask your child to copy it on the bottom.

If your child is ready, do the activity again with him drawing the picture on the top half and you drawing it on the bottom.

3. Rubbings

Objective: To teach your child coloring skills.

About the Game: Part of this activity teaches the skill of holding the paper steady and applying pressure with a crayon to make a design appear. The second part of this activity is to design a sheet of paper with interesting rubbing designs.

How to Play: Take out a quarter, dime, nickel, and penny. Ask your child to place them in random spots under an eight-and-a-half-by-eleven-inch sheet of paper. Then ask him to use a crayon and rub over the coins. Have fun trying to identify the coins as they appear. Continue the play placing the coins in different spots on the paper and rubbing over them with different color crayons. Take your turn doing some rubbings as well.

Another way to do rubbings is with leaves. Collect some from outside and make some interesting designs with those as well.

4. Color by Number

Objective: To teach your child how to color in the lines while doing a thoughtful activity.

About the Game: You can start with a simple drawing that has only two sections to it and gradually expand to a more complicated design with three, four, five, six, seven, eight, or more parts to it.

How to Play: Assign a number for each color you use on your design, and write a key for your child to follow. Instead of the color word, you can also put colored lines in your numbered key. Your child can do this activity all by himself, or you can take turns coloring by number. This is a detective type of activity. You can ask your child to find all the 1's, 2's, etc. As in other coloring activities, it is appropriate to emphasize coloring in the whole space and trying to leave no white space at all. It is also appropriate to expect different levels of coloring expertise from different children. Coloring skills improve over time.

5. Describing What to Draw

Objective: To teach your child drawing skills.

About the Game: You can tailor this activity to the drawing skills of your child.

How to Play: Fold an eight-and-a-half-by-eleven-inch sheet of paper in four parts. Number the sections 1, 2, 3, and 4. Describe to your child what to draw in each box. Your directions could range from being as simple as a sun or a flower to being as complicated as a house or garden. If your child is interested, he can do this same activity with you.

6. Scene Drawing

Objective: To teach your child drawing skills.

About the Game: Besides the drawing skills, your child will pick up visualization skills. These are important for listening and reading comprehension.

A lawn with green grass, trees, and flowers.

How to Play:　Give your child plain paper and crayons. Markers are fine for this activity as well. Then describe to your child a simple scene for him to draw. Here are some suggested examples:

- A lawn with green grass, a tree, and flowers.
- A table with flowers in a vase on it.
- A bookcase with books.

Writing

7. Follow the Dots

Objective:　To teach your child to write straight lines.

About the Game:　You can make follow-the-dots patterns quickly and easily and at the correct level of difficulty for your

Follow the dots.

child. You can use numbers or alphabet letters to label the dots. You can put them in random order or arrange them in specific designs.

How to Play: Make a follow-the-dots pattern for your child. Lead him through the activity as much as is necessary. Help him work toward doing the activity as independently as possible. After he is finished with a pattern, he may want to make a follow-the-dots design for you.

8. Tracing

Objective: To teach your child writing skills.

About the Game: Tracing paper, white copy paper, a paper clip, and index cards are needed for this activity.

How to Play: Write your child's initials or his name on the white copy paper. Choose whichever kind of writing is more suited to your child's writing skill level. If his initials are too hard, use a random combination of straight lines. If his name is too easy, write an interesting phrase or sentence. Then attach the tracing paper to the copy paper with a paper clip and ask your child to trace what is written on the white paper. If your child is interested, he can write something for you on a piece of white copy paper, and you can trace it on a piece of tracing paper.

Another way to do this tracing activity is by tracing on the white copy paper shapes cut from index cards or by tracing the whole index card itself. If you make an index card shape, you can cut it on the outside, forming the card into a new shape, or cut it on the inside to make it like a template.

A third variation is to trace on the white copy paper easily accessible household objects like blocks, cookie cutters, plastic cups, small bowls, and other items that you might find. You can take turns tracing these objects.

9. Following a Maze

Objective: To teach your child to write lines in a careful manner.

About the Game: When you make your own maze, you can tailor the difficulty of it to the level of your child. You can begin with a simple maze and make them more difficult as your child increases his skill.

How to Play: Draw a maze for your child. Ask him to get to the end without going out of the lines or crossing a line. The simplest can be a straight path, and the most complicated can be one with many choices. You can make up any story you like to go with your maze. Here are some examples:

- Help the dog find his bone.
- Help the boy find his house.
- Help the girl find her doll.

10. Making Patterns

Objective: To teach your child to make patterns accurately.

About the Game: Start with simple patterns and do more advanced ones later. Make them according to the level and interest of your child.

How to Play: Fold an eight-and-a-half-by-eleven-inch sheet of paper in half. Draw your pattern on the left-hand side of the paper and have your child copy the pattern on the right-hand side of the page. Start with a simple pattern with only three or four symbols in it. Use simple symbols like a circle, square, cross, letters, and numbers. If your child is successful copying a simple pattern, make the next pattern a little more difficult. If he is not successful with it, design an easier pattern.

Another way to play this game is by using a full eight-and-a-half-by-eleven-inch sheet of paper and describing your pattern instead of writing it as a model. In this case you would describe the relationship of the new items to the others. Here is an example of directions you might give for your child for drawing a pattern.

- Put a circle in the middle of the paper.

- Put two lines on either side of it.
- Put a circle next to the line on the left.
- Put an X next to the line on the right.

11. Crossing Out Letters

Objective: To teach your child to write letters.

About the Game: Going through the process of looking for letters adds interest to wanting to write them.

Write a simple sentence at the top of a plain piece of paper. Here are some suggested samples:

- Cynthia, you look pretty today.
- I like your new red dress.

How to Play: Tell your child to go on a letter treasure hunt and to circle all the A's in the sentences. Then tell him to be a detective and put an X on all the E's in the sentences. Go back to circling and ask for all the I's. Next is the X for all the O's. Last but not least will be a circle for all the U's. Then give the next instruction, which is to write each sentence over with the letters that are left without circles around them or X's on them.

12. Letter Writing

Objective: To give your child an opportunity to practice his writing as a communication skill.

Writing a letter.

About the Game: You can give your child as much or as little help as needed to get his message across. It is fine to ignore little mistakes and best to focus on clear letters or words and other small successes. It is also fine if you write the letter, and he helps you as much as he can.

How to Play: Check the next birthday or anniversary in your family, including grandparents, aunts, and uncles. Help your child write a short letter of congratulations. Guide him as necessary. If you and your child choose to write another kind of letter, a suggestion is to write one to your child. You or he can address the envelope, seal it, and put a stamp on it. You can take him to a mailbox to mail it. He will be delighted to see it postmarked and come back to him through the mail. As follow-up, it would be wonderful for you both to read the letter together.

13

Games for Listening

Because listening looks so passive, it is easy to ignore important developmental facets that are related to it. *Auditory discrimination* and *auditory memory* hold the key. These are definite experiences that contribute to this skill. The other broad terms that are connected with this area are *receptive language* and its partner term *comprehension*. Building receptive language and comprehension is the goal for activities connected with listening.

There are important skills of listening that will help you listen to your child. One is to look directly into his left eye as he talks. That gives you a stronger point of focus as you try to understand exactly what he is saying. Another is to be on his same level. That means you will do better if you bend down or sit on a low chair when he is speaking. A third idea is to be in the same physical position as your child to give him a feeling of compatibility.

Relative to communication and conversation with children, it is recommended to speak for 30 percent of the time and listen for 70 percent. To aid in this process there are words of communication that encourage your child to speak more to you. These are: "Oh, uh huh, good, and then," and "Tell me more about . . . ." There are also open-ended questions that are helpful, like: How did you do that? Why did that happen? What was that like? Please explain that further.

Look at the letters in these two words: LISTEN and SILENT. Yes, they are the same. It is interesting to ponder the relationship of these two actions:

- You are silent when you listen.
- People communicate through silence as well as through words.

"Listen" is defined in the *American Heritage Dictionary of the English Language* (p. 1049) as "To make an effort to hear something."

The following games are divided into the two areas that help to build listening skills—auditory discrimination and auditory memory.

Auditory Discrimination

1. Hide the Timer

Objective: To teach your child auditory discrimination.

About the Game: A kitchen timer that has a ticking sound is recommended for this game. A small music box or sound toy could be used as well.

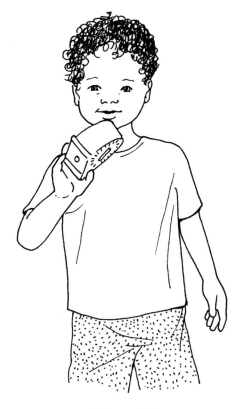

I found it!

How to Play: Take turns with your child. Start by hiding the timer, music box, or sound toy in another room. Have your child try to find it by following the sound. Once he finds it and brings it back to you in the first room, he can take it back to the other room and hide it for you to find.

2. Describe an Outfit

Objective: To teach your child auditory discrimination.

About the Game: Clothes are interesting to young children. Because they come in different colors, patterns, and styles, describing them provides an opportunity to use many different words.

How to Play: Open up your child's closet and stand with him a few feet away from the clothes. Without pointing to it, describe an outfit or item of clothing that you see. Ask your child to point to the one you just described. Keep adding details until your child can identify it correctly.

Once this game technique has become successful and fun, you can use it when you and your child are actually selecting an outfit or item of clothing for your child to wear. If your child is interested and when the time is appropriate, you can take the game to your closet and let your child describe an outfit or item of clothing for you to wear.

3. Red Light, Green Light

Objective: To teach your child auditory discrimination.

About the Game: This is an age-old children's game that has been passed down from generation to generation.

How to Play: Stand across the room from your child. Explain to your child that when you say "Red light," he is to stay still and that when you say "Green light," he can walk towards you. Explain that you will keep rotating between Red light and Green light and that he should listen carefully to the words so that he will know exactly what to do. There are other rules about being tagged by the leader that apply when you play in a big group, but those rules are not applicable to this parent-child game situation. After you finish one round, your child can be the leader and tell you "Red light," and "Green light," as you cross from one part of the room to the other.

4. Over, Under, Around, and Through

Objective: To teach your child auditory discrimination.

About the Game: You will need a doll and a chair for you and your child.

How to Play: Sit on chairs opposite each other. Then teach your child this little rhyme. Do it first by acting it out with your child and then by having your child act it out with a doll.

>   Over, under, around, and through.
>   That's not all that you can do.
>   In back of, in front of, at my side.
>   Watch my baby smile wide.

5. Stringing Beads

Objective: To teach your child auditory discrimination.

About the Game: Because large colorful beads are often easily accessible in the house of a young child, this medium is good for an auditory discrimination activity. You can start with a direction for two beads and expand to three and four as your child is ready. If beads are not available, you can use painted noodles, colored empty spools, or something else you find for stringing.

How to Play: Tell your child to string a few beads at a time in a certain order. Here are some examples:

- Blue and then red.
- Yellow, blue, and then red.
- Blue, yellow, green, and then red.

Keep adding colors to your directions up to a level of difficulty that is appropriate for your child. Then repeat the direction.

6. Rhymes

Objective: To teach your child auditory discrimination.

About the Game: Young children love rhyming words. Use a set of three-by-five-inch index cards for this game. Write a short word on one side and a rhyme on the other. Turn this into a guessing game.

How to Play: Take turns picking a card. Read the word on one side of the card, or let your child read it if he can. Then take turns trying to guess what the rhyming word is on the other side of the card. Here are some suggestions: say/day, bed/fed, big/wig, fog/log, man/tan, ten/men, hat/sat, hot/pot. Make up as many cards as you wish. When you are playing, you will find that there are many different rhyming words, in addition to the one shown, that rhyme with the matching word. Either write in the extra words that rhyme or be positive about any rhyming words that are said and have fun trying to guess the one that is written on the card.

Say, day, bed, fed.

Auditory Memory

7. The Directions Game

Objective: To teach your child auditory memory.

About the Game: You can start with two directions and then go on to three. The directions are to do actions that your child will enjoy. Because he has to hear all of them before following any one of them, he will be developing his auditory memory.

How to Play: Give your child directions to follow and ask him to do them in the order given. Here are some examples:

It's fun to follow directions.

- Touch the chair and then the sofa and then the door.
- Clap your hands, jump over a card, and then walk around me.
- Open the door, pat the table, and jump three times.

8. Call the Time

Objective: To teach your child auditory memory.

About the Game: In every area there is a local telephone number that you can dial to get the correct time. You can get this number from directory assistance. When your child calls this number, he is likely to hear an advertisement for a product, the temperature, and then the time. Call first to hear all that is being said. Because of all the other information, it may be difficult for your child to remember the time after he has hung up the phone. Besides asking your child to remember the time, you can present the challenge of trying to remember the temperature or other information as well.

How to Play: Dial the local number for the time or ask your child to do that if he can. Have him listen for the time so that he will be able to tell it to you after he hangs up. Then ask about the temperature. Then ask about other information he may remember. Your child is likely to get better and better at this the more times he plays.

9. Choosing Objects in a Room

Objective: To teach your child auditory memory.

About the Game: Choosing a category of items will make this memory game a little easier. Suggested categories are round, green, wooden, hard, soft, big, and small. You may think of others.

How to Play: Sit together on a comfortable couch or set of chairs, indoors or out. Take turns with your child naming objects in a selected category. Always repeat what has been said before you add your new item. Here is an example of the way it might work:

Child—Green cup.
Parent—Green cup and green vase.
Child—Green cup, green vase, and green dish.
Parent—Green cup, green vase, green dish, and green castle.

Name up to five items in the room in that category and then switch to a new category.

10. Telling What You Heard

Objective: To teach your child auditory memory.

About the Game: People love to talk about what they have done. It is very important to be able to listen well to other people. Being able to tell their story back to them shows that you have listened and remembered. This is a nice way to share experiences with one another.

How to Play: Sit together with your child in a quiet room in a quiet place. Take turns telling about something that happened to you during the day or about something that you have done. After you each take your turn, have the other person tell the story back. You can both feel free to make any additions or corrections to the story you hear back. Feel free to exchange all kinds of daily experiences.

11. Telling What Was Said

Objective: To teach your child auditory memory.

About the Game: Many things are said during the day that we hardly pay attention to but that we remember anyway. Often people remember different things that were said at a particular time or as part of a particular event. Once your child has played this game he is likely to pay more attention to what people are saying in different circumstances.

How to Play: Pick an event that you both experienced together. It could be something like eating lunch together, or it could be going to a movie or attending a special class or outing. Then take turns telling something that you heard someone say at that time. Here are some examples:

- Rachel's mother told Rachel to put on her shoes.
- Jennifer told me to move to the side.
- Aldo told Warren to give him a cracker.

12. Retelling a Story

Objective: To teach your child auditory memory.

About the Game: Read an interesting story to your child that you think your child could tell back to you. Some favorites that are fun to tell are "The Three Bears," *The Hungry Caterpillar* by Eric Carle, "The Three Little Kittens," *Green Eggs and Ham* by Dr. Seuss, and *Blueberries for Sal* by Robert McCloskey. You may have other favorites.

How to Play: Read the story to your child. Then ask him to tell it back to you.

I can tell the story.

14

Games for Speaking

Because speaking develops somewhat naturally, it is easy to think that it is not important to model high-quality language for children. However, that is farthest from the truth. A high quantity of quality speech is a necessity for your child. Then in addition to having this modeling, your child needs many opportunities to express himself. These need to be as part of conversations and also in terms of spontaneous self-expression. In general, young children make certain errors of speech and of grammar that they correct naturally over time. However, there is also a role that you can play that actually guides your child through that process. It is modeling correctly an incorrect word or words back to your child. Another thing you can do is expand beginning sentences your child says with more words and additional information. For example, when you hear, "The tree is big," you can say, "The tree is big with beautiful, green leaves."

Children develop speaking from activities in these three areas—hearing adults read to, sing to, and talk to them, joining in conversational dialogues with adults, and expressing themselves with different kinds of monologues.

"Speak" is defined in the *American Heritage Dictionary of the English Language* (p. 1729) as "To utter words or articulate sounds with ordinary speech modulation; talk."

The following games come from these three areas of speech—receptive language, conversation, and expressive language.

Receptive Language

1. Read a Book to Your Child

Objective: To teach your child receptive vocabulary.

About the Game: Reading to your child is for the purpose of having him understand the content.

How to Play: Select a book that you think your child will both enjoy and understand. Read it sentence-by-sentence or paragraph-by-paragraph to your child. After each sentence or after each paragraph either explain what it means or ask your child if he knows. Keep in mind that you are communicating ideas, thoughts, and information and not testing your child or putting him on the spot in any way. Many books have ideas, thoughts, and information in them that are over the heads of children and need to be explained. You might even find specific vocabulary words that need to be made clear.

Do you understand?

2. New Words to an Old Song

Objective: To teach your child receptive vocabulary.

About the Game: You can teach a lot of new vocabulary by substituting new words in old songs. Here are some ideas:

- Old MacDonald Had a House, Car, Yard, etc.
- The Great Big Spider
- Drive, Drive, Drive Your Car

How to Play: Choose a song that you both know well. Have your child sit on your lap or next to you in a comfortable place, like on a sofa or in a big easy chair. Sing freely together. Make up new songs like these as you think of them.

3. Talk to Your Child about Your Childhood

Objective: To teach your child receptive vocabulary.

About the Game: Children always enjoy hearing about when their parents were children. This topic will give you a chance to talk a lot to your child at a relatively high level and with high-interest information.

How to Play: Find a comfortable place to sit together. It might be on a sofa or in a big easy chair. Begin with a question like, What would you like to know about what it was like when I was a child? You will probably get many questions. Answer them in whatever way you wish. Enjoy this time to share this special information.

4. Talking to Your Child about You

Objective: To teach your child receptive vocabulary.

About the Game: Children have a lot of curiosity about their parents' life and work. While this was always so, it is even more pronounced today because most parents spend a great many hours away from their children. Just as with the game Talk to Your Child about Your Childhood, this game will give you a chance to talk a lot to your child at a relatively high level and with high-interest information.

How to Play: Take your child to a special place in your house where you do some form of work. If you have a home office, that would be fine. If you have a desk area, that is good too. Maybe you work a lot on a bed or in a big chair. Wherever you have a place where you concentrate will be good for this activity.

Find a place in this area that is comfortable for you and your child. Then ask your child something like, What would you like to know about my life or work? As with the Talk to Your Child about Your Childhood game, you will probably get many questions. Answer them with as much information as possible. Explain whatever you do as much on your child's level as possible. Enjoy this time to share this special information.

Conversation

5. Talking about Pictures

Objective: To teach your child skills of self-expression.

About the Game: Your child may enjoy cutting out colorful pictures from magazines. If not, cut out an assortment of people in many different settings.

How to Play: Take turns picking a picture and describing it. Here are a few examples:

- A mother out in a field holding her child.
- A mother at home playing with a baby.
- Two children acting out parts in a play.

Then have fun asking each other the "W" questions—Who, What, Where, When, and Why?

- Who is in the picture?

- What are they doing?
- Where are they?
- When does this take place?
- Why are they there?

6. The Conversation

Objective: To teach your child skills of self-expression.

About the Game: Often mealtime is a good setting for a conversation. You can have this conversation at a planned mealtime if only you two will be present, or you can set it up at a special snack time that you share together.

How to Play: Begin your meal with pleasant words like "Bon appétit" or "Hearty appetite." Then let the conversation flow. Listen, talk, enjoy, and see where the conversation takes you. In today's busy times, this opportunity for your child to have your complete attention should be quite rewarding.

7. Walking Hand in Hand

Objective: To teach your child skills of self-expression.

About the Game: Taking a walk together is another way to enjoy conversation. This is different than walking quickly to a destination where something needs to be accomplished.

How to Play: Go for a walk with your child. Stroll hand in hand in a relaxed manner, and you are likely to see the conversation flow.

Tell me more about your day.

8. Block Building or Related Sets

Objective: To teach your child skills of self-expression.

About the Game: Use any building set you may have. Some possibilities are wooden blocks, plastic blocks, Bristle Blocks, Tinkertoys, Lincoln Logs, Lego, bottle caps, or any other set for building. Sharing in a creative activity like this is an effective way to stimulate conversation.

How to Play: Set up your building activity in a quiet area. Then begin creating together. Talk about what you are doing or about any other subjects that become natural conversation. Enjoy this special time together.

Hand in hand.

Expressive Language

9. Vocabulary-Building Words

Objective: To teach your child expressive vocabulary.

About the Game: Vocabulary building can be effective in a game format.

How to Play: Make a list of items that can be called by a different name. Then choose one word at a time and take turns thinking of another word for that word. Here is an example of how play might go: pants—jeans, cup—mug, shirt—tank top, hat—cap. Some words will have several choices. For example, for pants you could also have shorts, trousers, and leggings. Here are suggested words for this kind of play: coat, shoe, road, car, rock, plate, laptop, and silverware. You may be able to think of others.

Another variation of this game is naming words that go in specific categories. You can take turns naming words that go in a particular category. For example, one category is fruit. You can take turns naming fruits like apple, pear, banana, grapes, orange, pineapple, apricot, and plum. There are many more. Here are other suggested categories: vegetables, cars, trees, flowers, and animals. Again, there are many more.

10. Finishing the Story

Objective: To teach your child expressive vocabulary.

About the Game: As your child gets older, he will make more elaborate stories.

How to Play: Start telling a story and then ask your child to finish it. Here are some story starters:

- Mother brought home five bags of groceries. What happened next?
- The children were playing out in the yard, and then it started to rain. What happened next?
- Father lit the barbecue. What happened next?

11. Poem, Song, or Nursery Rhyme

Objective: To teach your child expressive language.

About the Game: Performing a poem, nursery rhyme, or song should be fun for your child and also serve to raise his self-esteem.

How to Play: Start off saying and singing together some familiar poems, rhymes, and songs. Some favorites are "Roses are Red," "Little Boy Blue," "Mary Had a Little Lamb," "Three Blind Mice," "Twinkle, Twinkle Little Star," and "Row, Row, Row Your Boat." You may know others that both you and your child would enjoy experiencing. After your child is comfortable performing with you, see if he would like to say or sing one of them on his own.

12. The Explanation

Objective: To teach your child expressive language.

About the Game: You will need props for this activity. Here are some that are often easily found at home: flashlight, paintbrush, broom, sponge, pencil or pen, book, hairbrush, plate, and toothbrush.

How to Play: Make a collection of these kinds of items and put them in a plastic shopping bag. Then take turns picking an item. When you take out your item, explain how you use it or how it is used. If it is a flashlight, you can bring the other person over to a dark corner and show how it lights up. If it is a pen or pencil, you can go get a piece of paper and write with it.

Look in here!

Have fun explaining these simple items to each other. If you think your child has not expressed himself clearly, you can ask him a question about the item or ask him to tell you more about it. In addition, tell your child that he can also ask you questions about the objects you pick.

PART FIVE

The Home
Environment

Your home is your family's castle. Therefore, make it magnificent for all your family members. Something as simple as colors can make a difference. Blue has a calming effect, and yellow raises the energy level. Music works the same way. Soft classical music soothes the soul, and loud popular music makes you more frenetic. Try to reduce clutter as much as possible. That too will help to make home life run more smoothly.

"Make your home as inviting as possible. Make your home a place where your family loves to be. Try to allow as much natural sunlight into your home as possible. Sunlight is very therapeutic for a person's state of mind. Keep your home as spacious and open as possible. Try to surround yourself and your family with what pleases all of you" (Granitur, p. 16).

"Make your home as calm as possible. Your home is where you should be able to relax and enjoy your family. You and your family will be able to find a mental and spiritual balance if your home is calm. Try to think positive thoughts which will in turn put out positive energy in your home." (Granitur, p. 15).

Schedules fit right in with this concept as well. They provide a way to help everyone know what is expected of them and when to take care of their responsibilities. How you set up the atmosphere will stay with your children forever. Parenting is how you carry it out. It has great power.

Knowing how important your home life is, you can even make a mission statement for your family and display it proudly. It could include thoughts about being a good, positive family in which each member leads a healthy life. It could include having courteous behavior and high integrity. It could have whatever you want it to have. You can play with your own thoughts and ideas and create one that fits your family just right. The helpful part is having it visible for all to see as a form of guidance for each family member each and every day. A suggestion is to post it in a place where you and other family members can add to it other motivational messages related to this mission. This kind of process is similar to a vision for a business. It is hard to "get there" if you do not know "exactly where you are going."

Make your home like a garden of love. Take the best care possible of the flowers within it. The water, sunshine, and fertilizer of life will help each person in it bloom to magnificence. There will always be problems that come up as part of daily living, but each family member should know that he or she can turn to any family member at any time for nurturing love, guidance, support, and protection.

15

| Set the table. | Sweep the floor. | Dust the furniture. |

An Enriched Learning Environment

You Are the Number One Teacher

In your home you are the number one teacher. "They will do what you do and not what you say" is a well-known statement in the field of child development. Your job as a parent is like that of a director. While the end goal is for your child to be able to function well on his own, he will need much guidance through the years to get to that point. The idea is to interact with your child in a positive way, model behavior, explain how to do many things, and at the same time be careful not to be constantly correcting or too critical.

The games presented in this book provide a structure for demonstrating a style of leadership. They can be used in the game situation and then also as reminders of how to teach important skills that come up from day to day.

"Home is where the heart is" is another well-known statement. Because a home is basically set up for adults, with everything in it of adult-size, you need to try to think of all the ways you can modify it so that it is child-size as well. A coffee table that is low for you can be a regular-size table for your child if used with low stools as chairs. Bulletin boards and pictures in your child's room, usually placed at an adult's eye level, can be lowered. Check around your house to see if you can lower hooks for your child to hang his own things on and if you can lower some closet racks for him to hang up his own clothes. For high closet racks in your child's room you might want to make a sturdy step stool available. Check his drawers and shelves to see if they are set up so that they are easy for your child to manage.

Besides checking your physical house, check your mental world. As you go through experiences, keep thinking of ways to explain them to your child on the appropriate level. He is constantly learning about the world and tying to figure it out, and you can help him by giving clear explanations. Moreover, sharing this important information will provide you with a rewarding experience as well.

You are your child's number one teacher. Because you know him better than anyone else, that makes you the best one for teaching and explaining many things. The insight you have about your child from your love and the many hours you spend together is what makes you such an expert.

Because of our fast-moving way of life, we spend hours en route and then even more hours waiting once we arrive at places like doctor's offices and restaurants. Many of the games in this book are applicable while en route and others while you are waiting. All of the games give you a way to teach as you play.

Helping Around the House

Introduce your child to as many jobs around the house as possible. He wants to be helpful. He will have more meaning in his life by participating than by having everything done for him. Try to find easy responsibilities at first and continue to add new ones as he grows. Sorting and folding clothes, including matching socks, are good starters. Clearing dishes and later setting the table are also appropriate. Any help in cooking like mixing, measuring, and pouring can be taught. Dusting and sweeping are also possibilities.

Show your child where everything goes in his room. Ask him to be as responsible as possible for his belongings. Try to teach work in the house as positive fun. Bring out the satisfaction of doing a job well and taking care of oneself and one's things. If there are several jobs to do, you can make it into a game activity. Write each job on a separate index card and then have fun picking a card to see which job comes up first. Here are some examples:

- Sweep the floor.
- Dust the furniture.
- Clean a mirror.
- Set the table.
- Tidy a drawer.

Place the cards in a pile. Then ask your child to pick a card and read it. You can help with the reading as much as is needed. Adding this element of surprise will add fun to the task. If possible, work on the task together. This kind of playing and working together will help you both to experience a meaningful, growing, positive relationship. While sharing and teaching should be part of your regular routine, it is not necessary for you and your child to do everything together. You will find that you can do some jobs more easily and efficiently by yourself. However, as many activities as possible are worth a try.

A Few Words about Nutrition

Proper nutrition plays as important a role in the home environment of your child as his physical surroundings and activities. The key concept is a balanced diet of whole foods, avoiding artificial colors, flavors, and preservatives. The idea is to keep him away from processed foods as much as possible. It is also important to start these kinds of eating habits as early as possible. Healthful eating at this stage will lead to healthful eating as an adult and will play a major role in lessening the likelihood of your child developing the serious diseases that have become so prevalent in our culture.

Just as your child needs a balanced program of active and quiet activities, creative and routine ones, so he needs to eat according to the USDA (United States Department of Agriculture) Food Pyramid. The majority of the food on the pyramid is made up of whole grains, fruits, and vegetables. The minority is made up of meats, fish, poultry, dairy products, and fat. The meals each day do not have to be perfectly aligned according to the pyramid, but if you notice the same imbalance day after day, you can then change the diet.

A Few Words about Exercise

Proper exercise plays as important a role in your child's life as nutrition. The key concept is planning it on a regular basis. It is not enough to leave it to chance. There is too much time today that children are sedentary—in classrooms, watching television and videos, playing with a computer, and riding in a car. Therefore, it is important to have a regularly scheduled exercise routine for your child or for you and your child together. It could be at home, at a park, or as part of an organized program like gymnastics, karate, a sport, ballet, or something like that. It is important to start these exercise habits as soon as possible. Regular exercise at this stage will lead to regular exercise as an adult and will play a major role in maintaining excellent health.

Just as your child needs to eat according to the USDA Food Pyramid, so he needs to have a full program of stretches, aerobic activity, and muscle-development exercises. You can do simple body stretches with your child that will probably be fun for both of you. Then running around for aerobics will probably happen naturally. Sit-ups, recommended in the crunch position, for muscle development are another suggestion. Lifting weights with items like soup cans or half-pound bags of sugar are also well-liked. There are also excellent CDs available for children's exercises that have kids follow along with a trained exercise instructor.

A Few Words about Sleep

Proper sleep plays as important a role in your child's life as nutrition and exercise. As a matter of fact, according to research done by Professor James Maas from Cornell University, proper sleep is the single most important determinant in predicting longevity. It is more important than nutrition, exercise, and even heredity. While sleep looks like it is a passive activity, it is actually active. The sleep process directly affects health, happiness, and performance.

While you sleep, your body is busy at work rejuvenating its entire system. For an adult it takes an average of eight hours.

For children, it takes an average of ten to eleven. Sleep affects alertness, communication skills, energy, learning, mood, and thinking. The key concept is planning sleep on a regular basis. It is not enough to leave it to chance. It is most beneficial to your child's body when sleep is on a schedule. His body has a natural clock and rhythm for sleeping, and that rhythm should be nurtured.

A sleep schedule is similar to an eating schedule. It should be regular and be more or less at the same time each day. Just as with meals, hours of sleep will vary slightly according to a daily schedule, but they should never be missed. Some days your child might eat a little more and on others a little less, but there should always be a plan for well-rounded healthy nutrition. Sleep should follow the same concept of variability within the context of a consistent sleep schedule.

It is important to start these sleep habits as early as possible. Regular sleep at this stage will play a major roll in leading to regular sleep as an adult and also in maintaining excellent health. Part of the sleep routine should include explaining the positive value of sleep. Explaining to your child that sleep provides a wonderful part of the day for rest and rejuvenation will actually help him to want to go to sleep. In addition, sharing with him the idea that if he is well rested during the night that he will be able to do better at everything he does during the following day also helps with the sleep routine.

Here are some of the benefits of a regular schedule of about ten to eleven hours of sleep a night:

- High motivation and the ability to stick to a task.
- Being cooperative.

Here are some of the problems that occur from not enough sleep:

- Mental lapses or micro sleeps. Your child will easily fall asleep while reading, writing, and watching television and videos.
- Distractibility, impulsivity, and difficulty concentrating.
- Crankiness, anger, aggressiveness, irritability, impatience, and low tolerance for frustration.
- Exacerbation of ADD or ADHD symptoms.

To have a successful bedtime, you need to set up a strict routine. A routine is difficult to enforce in today's busy times. However, believing in it is the most important factor in being able to make it happen. Keep the power. If you know it is important, you will feel confident in what you are doing. If you feel confident, your actions will show it, and that will make your child likely to follow your lead.

Here are some tried and tested bedtime routine suggestions:

- Soft music.
- Reading.
- Soft toys for play.
- Explaining sleep benefits.
- Quiet, cool, uncluttered, and dark room.
- High-quality mattress and pillow.
- Warm bath.
- Easy stretching.
- Speaking away worries.
- Mental imagery.
- Meditation.

Experts advise that you have your child make up for lost sleep. It is like a bank. If you take money out of it, you need to put money back into it. Value this aspect of your child's life as much as you do his full nutrition requirements and his daily exercise. Teach your child the beauty behind his magnificent body and the special care it needs every day in terms of excellent nutrition, exercise, and sleep.

Your Child's Birthday

The moment of birth has been a cause for celebration in every culture and since the beginning of time. Each and every baby is different. Each one will grow in his own unique way. Then each year that goes by is a celebration of life and a year of growth. On the one hand it is a reflection of many past accomplishments. On the other, it carries with it new responsibilities for your child and the idea of being capable of new achievements.

The Birthday Party

A birthday party is the most popular way in which to celebrate a child's birthday. Because your child looks forward to this special day for a long time, you have the responsibility of trying to plan appropriate activities that will make that day as meaningful as possible. The rule of thumb for children's parties is to invite one more child than the age of the child. For example, if he is five, you invite six children. If he is four, you invite five. Very often you have other social obligations and cannot abide by this rule, but it seems to work well if you can manage it.

While it is nice to have children's parties in restaurants, children's theaters, parks, and other special-event places, for a young child who is first learning what a party is, there is no place like home. The simple traditions are worthwhile to teach before you change and elaborate on them as you might do for an older child.

Here are some birthday-party activities that are easy to prepare and that will be meaningful for a young child. You can expand the concepts for an older child who can do a little more. These activities do not include competition; they focus on participation.

Stickers on a Present.   You can wrap up a favor for each child, the same or similar kind for everyone and place a different sticker on each package. One at a time, give each child a card with a sticker on it that matches a sticker on a present. The child can then correctly match the card to the present. After everyone makes their matches, they can all open their presents and place their discarded wrapping in a central carton, bag, or pail.

Pass the Present.   Also known as Pass the Parcel, this game is similar to the well-known "hot potato" game. Tell all the children to sit in a circle. As you play music they pass a present wrapped in many layers of gift wrap. When you stop the music, the child who has the present opens one layer of wrap. When you start the music, the children continue to pass it. You continue in this way until the present is completely unwrapped. The present should be something that has a piece for every player, like a group of children's rings, bracelets, notepads, and so on, so often available as party favors in party stores.

Color Happy Birthday.   Write out Happy Birthday in large, thick letters that can be colored in on a large paper tablecloth. Write the name of each of the guests in one or more of the letters. They can then color the letters that are designated with their own names.

All these activities go well with a good serving of cake and ice cream and a simple lunch if you desire. No candy is necessary for their pleasure. Because of all the exposure to junk food in daily life, a birthday party is a great time to treat the children to natural food of the highest quality. Here are some ideas:

- Fresh fruits displayed with their beautiful, bright colors.
- Cheese pieces cut to easily go on crackers.
- Vegetables cut in an attractive manner to go with a delicious dip.
- Fruit juices.
- Small pita sandwiches with hummus, tomatoes, and sprouts.
- Peanut butter and cream cheese spread on bread and cut in interesting shapes with cookie-cutter forms.
- Small cups of natural yogurt with granola sprinkled on top.

Acting to Children's Songs.   There are several CDs that children can enjoy by following along with actions. A good selection is often found in specialty educational stores. Explain to the children before you play it what it is going to be like. An alternative to this kind of action CD is to play a CD or popular song on the radio that is good for dancing.

Activities with Blocks and Puzzles.   If you have a large quantity of any one kind of blocks, introduce them as a play activity. Judge by the age and size of your group what kinds and numbers of blocks would be appropriate. After they play freely for a

Happy Birthday.

while, ask them to build something specific like a train, tower, or castle. For puzzles, give each child his own. If you have enough, set them up as partners. You can set a timer and see who can complete their puzzle before the timer rings. You might want to do another round after switching the puzzles.

The Acting Game.   There are lots of different categories of actions you can write out on a group of index cards, one action per card. You could use animals, careers, or action words or phrases. In turn, each child picks a card and acts out what it says. If the children are old enough, you could show one child his card secretly. Then as he acts it out, the other children can try to guess what the card said. Here are some examples. You could make up many, many more.

Animals	Careers	Actions
Dog	Police Officer	Hop
Cat	Fire Fighter	Jump
Elephant	Teacher	Clap
Horse	Doctor	Sing
Cow	Secretary	Eat Food
Pig	Bus Driver	Drive a Car

Talent Show.   Ask each child in turn to sing a song, dance, or do some special gymnastics. Clap for each participant.

Party Favors.   A good party favor is a simple plastic beach ball. They are inexpensive. If the weather and time permit, you could take the children outside with their beach balls, help them blow them up, and play with all of their balls at one time. Other good presents are interesting notepads, crayons, puzzles, books, and play dough.

I invite you to celebrate your child's birthday with gusto. Celebrate it in your own special way. When you start thinking about presents to give your child, select the gift of your choice. Then as you reflect on the gift, remember about the gift of life and your child's magnificent growth and development. Remember to tell your child about that as well.

From special days like birthdays to every day, there are many worthwhile, interesting, and enjoyable activities to do with children. I hope that the suggested games in this book will provide you and your child with many happy hours of playing and learning together.

16

Working with Teachers

The Preschool Experience

As parent of your child, you are the specialist. You know more about him than anyone else does. Your child's preschool teachers will do all they can to get to know your child so that they can guide and support him through these developmental years, but you are the one who knows him the best.

Preschool is exactly what it says—pre-school. It is a place where your child can go to spend time in an interesting and productive manner in the years before he is developmentally ready for formal schooling. It is where he will have an opportunity to be with many children of and around his own age and where he will be exposed to activities that are appropriate for his age.

Preschool in Perspective

Preschool is one of the important experiences your child will have during these important years. However, it is not the most important one. The most important one is the family. Although he may gain some values, information, love, and support from preschool teachers, he will gain most of those from his home. He may feel connected to the preschool and to the teachers, but he will feel most connected to you and his family. No matter how much like home and how much like a family the preschool environment seems to be, it is not home, and it is not family; and it cannot provide the love, peace, and security that only a home and family can.

Finding a Preschool

There is no one set of directions for this situation. Every family has their own needs for child care. Proximity to your home or work, cost, and the program or curriculum all factor into the decision. However, with all of these factors, the key to finding a place is looking for one that most closely resembles an optimal home environment: a place with loving, caring parents who take every opportunity to care for and enrich the life of their child, a place where grandparents, aunts, uncles, and cousins do all kinds of supportive activities—active and quiet, educational and routine, firm and nurturing.

As you know, it is hard to create such an optimal home environment in this day and age. Many homes have parts of these elements but few, if any, have all of them. Therefore, one main reason for turning to a preschool is to look for a substitute in a preschool setting. It is caregivers of all kinds who take the place of grandparents, aunts, and uncles, and it is children in the preschool environment who take the place of cousins.

Teachers and Parents as Partners

The idea is to work with teachers as partners. Just as you would let members of your extended family play their natural roles with your child, so you can let the teachers. However, just as you would be totally in charge of your child, his activities, and whereabouts when with other family members, so you need to be totally in charge when you bring your child to preschool.

Help and Support

Allow the preschool and teachers to help and support you in your role as parent but be careful not to let them take over. Find out information from them that can help you as you love, nurture, and socialize your child but do not leave important decisions or daily child guidance in their hands. It is easy to make the mistake of believing that, because teachers are trained in child care and are knowledgeable about children, they can do a better job of parenting than you can. That is not the case. A teacher may be well trained and knowledgeable, but you as the parent know best.

The Parent and Teacher Roles

By this stage your child is becoming more and more acclimated to adult life and daily schedules. Learn as much as you can about the preschool day so that you can factor it into the big picture related to your child's health and well-being.

Here are areas of concern: nutrition, exercise, sleep, educational stimulation, and emotional support. Keep these areas in your view at all times so that you can continue to make sure that your child has a full and meaningful program in all of these areas throughout the day, week, and year.

Ready for School

During the preschool years is when you will be getting your child ready for school. It is quite a natural process that takes place for a child when he has these four elements present in his life:

- Fair, firm, and positive guidance and support.
- Responsive adults providing for his daily care.
- An educationally stimulating environment.
- A rich language environment.

It should be no surprise when you find your child ready for school. While children develop at different rates, there are clear markers that signal when a child is ready. Here are some well-accepted indications that will let you know. He should:

- Know his first and last names.
- Be able to tell his address.
- Be able to recite his telephone number.
- Know his parents' or guardians' names.
- Be able to catch a large ball most of the time.
- Be able to run and stop on signal.
- Be able to hop on one foot and skip.

- Be able to hold a pencil correctly.
- Be able to use scissors correctly.
- Like to tell riddles and jokes.
- Be able to copy shapes (circles, squares, triangles, and rectangles).
- Be able to sort by color, shape, and kind.
- Be able to fill in the missing part on pictures (of people, figures, animals, or houses).

The Preschool Years

This is an exciting time for you and your child. It is the time you have to share in a rich program of activities. You can arrange it so that some valuable activities will take place at the preschool. You can also arrange it so that much of it takes place in your home. There are no rules. Every child, parent, and family is different. The important thing is that you are aware of what goes on during these years and that you as the parent play the most significant role in setting up your child for success in school.

With not a moment to waste in providing your child with all the love and care he needs, you now have *Make Your Own Preschool Games*. Each chapter first explains about educational growth and development in a particular category. Then each one has twelve games that you and your child can enjoy together. The games are designed in such a way that while you both are having an enjoyable play experience and having the opportunity to build your own special positive relationship, your child will be learning at the same time. Whether you are playing a series of short games or are playing one of the longer ones, you can rest assured your child will be growing with the games.

Information for Making Game Cards

Game Category: To be written on the back side of each card.
Game title with page number reference: To be written on the front of each card.

Game Category: Mathematics

Game titles with page number references:

Game Category: Science

Game titles with page number references:

1. The Scientific Method, p. 25
2. Three Little Plants, p. 27
3. Paste a Pasta, p. 28
4. Sink or Float, p. 29
5. Make Your Own Bubbles, p. 30
6. Ball Roll, p. 31
7. Nature and Not, p. 31
8. The Solar System, p. 32
9. The Breath of Life, p. 35
10. Animals and Plants, p. 36
11. A Technology Hunt, p. 37
12. Computer Time, p. 38

Game Category: Social Studies

Game titles with page number references:

1. Me Box, p. 41
2. Educational Display, p. 41
3. My Family Collage, p. 43
4. My Friends, p. 43
5. When I Was Your Age, p. 44
6. Time Line, p. 45
7. Play and Say, p. 46
8. Row, Row, Row Your Boat, p. 47
9. Story of the Day, p. 48
10. Please and Thank You, p. 49
11. I Can . . . , p. 49
12. I Like . . . , p. 50

Game Category: Gross Motor Development

Game titles with page number references:

1. Warm Up, Cool Down, p. 60
2. Exercise Stations, p. 60
3. Moving and Dancing to the Music, p. 62
4. The X-ercise, p. 62
5. Pillow Pulls, p. 63
6. Child Olympics, p. 63
7. Sit-ups and Push-ups, p. 65
8. Hokey Pokey, p. 65
9. Mother, or Father, May I, p. 66
10. Simon Says, p. 67
11. Bowling, p. 68
12. Tennis, p. 69

Game Category: Fine-Motor Development

Game titles with page number references:

1. Play Dough, Clay, or Putty, p. 72
2. The Last Straw, p. 74
3. Where is Thumbkin?, p. 75
4. Building Toys, p. 76
5. Tearing and Pasting Paper, p. 76
6. Button Practice, p. 77
7. Itsy Bitsy Spider, p. 78
8. Lacing a Shoe, p. 80
9. The Tossing Game, p. 80
10. Potato Carry, p. 81
11. Lifting Weights, p. 82
12. Zip, p. 82

Game Category: Midline Development

Game titles with page number references:

1. Cross the Midline, p. 86
2. Checkerboard Patterns, p. 87
3. Follow the Yarn, p. 88
4. Eye Exercise, p. 89
5. Arms Together Side-to-Side, p. 89
6. Jack-in-the-Box, p. 90
7. Midline Matching, p. 92
8. Roll a Ball, p. 93
9. Leg and Arm Balance, p. 94
10. Row, Row, Row Your Boat, p. 95
11. Jumping Jacks, p. 95
12. Patty Cake, p. 96

Game Category: Social Skills

Game titles with page number references:

1. The Please Game, p. 104
2. The Thank You Game, p. 105
3. Working Together, p. 106
4. Play a Game, p. 106
5. I Like . . . , p. 107
6. My Favorite, p. 108
7. Just Like Me, p. 109
8. Foods, Toys, and Animals, p. 110
9. Cooking Together, p. 110
10. Putting Toys Away, p. 112
11. Doll Play, p. 113
12. Reflecting Together, p. 114

Game Category: Art

Game titles with page number references:

1. Crayon Play, p. 117
2. Pass the Art, p. 117
3. Paint, p. 118
4. Chalk, p. 119
5. Sculpting in the Kitchen, p. 119
6. Coil Pottery, p. 120
7. Flat Shapes, p. 120
8. Molding, p. 121
9. Masks, p. 123
10. Butterflies, p. 123
11. Appreciating Art, p. 124
12. Place Mats, p. 125

Game Category: Music

Game titles with page number references:

1. Classical Music of Your Choice, p. 129
2. Children's Music of Your Choice, p. 130
3. Drawing to Music, p. 131
4. Sing-along, p. 132
5. Singing to Your Child, p. 132
6. Make Up Songs, p. 133
7. Dancing, p. 134
8. Dancing to Directions, p. 135
9. Dancing Songs, p. 136
10. Simple Musical Instruments, p. 136
11. Homemade Musical Instruments, p. 137
12. Sophisticated Instruments, p. 137

Game Category: Drama

Game titles with page number references:

1. Going Out, p. 140
2. Dressing for the Occasion, p. 142
3. The Bedtime Plan, p. 143
4. The Restaurant, p. 144
5. The Health Club, p. 145
6. The Doctor's Office, p. 146
7. Making a Tent, p. 147
8. Using a Blanket, p. 148
9. Puppets, p. 150
10. Act Out a Book, p. 150
11. Nursery Rhyme Dramatics, p. 151
12. Acting Songs, p. 151

Game Category: Reading

Game titles with page number references:

1. Letter Cards, p. 158
2. Alphabet Song, p. 159
3. Alphabet Song II, p. 160
4. Word Cards, p. 161
5. Hop, Jump, and Clap, p. 163
6. Word Labels, p. 164
7. This is a . . . , p. 164
8. Message, p. 166
9. Short Directions, p. 167
10. Bookshelf Books, p. 167
11. A Reading Book, p. 168
12. Child's Magazine, p. 169

Game Category: Writing

Game titles with page number references:

1. Copy and Color in Shapes, p. 172
2. Picture Copying, p. 173
3. Rubbings, p. 174
4. Color by Number, p. 174
5. Describing What to Draw, p. 175
6. Scene Drawing, p. 175
7. Follow the Dots, p. 176
8. Tracing, p. 177
9. Following a Maze, p. 178
10. Making Patterns, p. 179
11. Crossing Out Letters, p. 180
12. Letter Writing, p. 180

Game Category: Listening

Game titles with page number references:

1. Hide the Timer, p. 184
2. Describe an Outfit, p. 185
3. Red Light, Green Light, p. 186
4. Over, Under, Around, and Through, p. 187
5. Stringing Beads, p. 187
6. Rhymes, p. 188
7. The Directions Game, p. 189
8. Call the Time, p. 190
9. Choosing Objects in a Room, p. 191
10. Telling What You Heard, p. 192
11. Telling What Was Said, p. 192
12. Retelling a Story, p. 193

Game Category: Speaking

Game titles with page number references:

Bibliography

Ayers, A. J. *Sensory Integration and the Child*. Los Angeles: Weskin Psychological Services, 1979.

Campbell, D. *The Mozart Effect, Music for Children: Relax, Daydream, and Draw*. Vol. 2. Audiocassette. Boulder, Colo.: The Children's Group, 1997.

Doman, G. *How to Teach Your Baby to Read*. Garden City, N.Y.: Doubleday and Co., 1975.

Education Publications Center (ED Pubs). *Helping Your Child Learn Math*. Washington, D.C.: U.S. Department of Education, 1999.

Gellens, S. *Activities That Build the Young Child's Brain*. Sarasota, Fla.: Early Childhood Association of Florida, Inc., 2000.

Goldberg, S. *Baby and Toddler Learning Fun*. Cambridge, Mass.: Perseus Publishing, 2001.

_____. *Growing with Games*. Ann Arbor, Mich.: University of Michigan Press, 1986.

_____. *Parent Involvement Begins at Birth*. Needham Heights, Mass.: Allyn & Bacon, 1997.

_____. *Teaching with Toys*. Ann Arbor, Mich.: University of Michigan Press, 1981.

Granitur, E. *I Love You Daddy*. Miami Beach, Fla.: Sydney's Sproutin' Company, 1996.

Gregg. E. M. *What to Do When "There's Nothing to Do."* New York: Dell Publishing Co., 1968.

Kay, E. *Games That Teach for Children Three through Six*. Minneapo-
lis: T. S. Denison and Co., 1981.

Lorton, M. B. *Workjobs: Activity-Centered Learning for Early Childhood Education*. Menlo Park, Calif.: Addison Wesley Publishing
Co., 1972.

Maas, J., Ph.D. *Power Sleep*. New York: Harper Perennial, 1999.

Moche, D. L. *My First Book about Space: A Question and Answer
Book*. Racine, Wisc.: Western Publishing Company, Inc., 1982.

Soukhanov, A. H., ed. *American Heritage Dictionary of the English
Language*. Boston: Houghton Mifflin Company, 1992.

Suzuki, S. *Nurtured by Love: The Classic Approach to Talent Education*. Smithtown, N.Y.: Exposition Press, 1982.

Index

Printed in the United States
151793LV00003B/38/A